Contents

Test 1

Paper 1 Reading and Writing (1 hour 30 minutes)

Reading
Part 1

Tip
Read the instructions and example, then do each question one at a time as there is no connection between them.

Questions 1–5

Look at the text in each question.
What does it say?
Mark the correct letter **A, B** or **C** on your answer sheet.

Example:

0

> **Use these doors only
> in an emergency.**

A   You must never leave by these doors.

B   The doors can be used if necessary.

C   Only some people can use these doors.

Answer:

1

> **After opening, keep in a
> refrigerator and use within
> two days.**

A   This product doesn't need to be kept cool.

B   This product can last for two days after you open it.

C   This product must be put in a refrigerator immediately.

2

> **The summer swimming
> timetable has changed. Please
> ask at reception for details.**

A   You can get information about new times from the receptionist.

B   Tell the receptionist about any change in your details.

C   The swimming pool is open at the usual times.

PET

PRACTICE TESTS

DATE DUE

2 3 JUN 2023	
	Y 2016
11.	
	R 2016
16 N	R 2016
12 0	AY 2015
	Y 2016
2 2 I	
2 5	2016
0 8	2016
	R 2018
	N 2019
	R 2020

PRINTED IN U.S.A.

Please return/renew this item by the last date shown

Tillibh/ath-chlaraidh seo ron cheann-latha mu dheireadh

PET Overview

Paper 1 Reading / Writing

Reading

Part	Task Type and Focus	No. of items	Task Format
1	Three-option multiple choice Reading real-world notices for main message.	5	Five short discrete texts: signs and messages, postcards, notes, emails, labels, etc.
2	Matching Reading multiple texts for specific information and detailed comprehension.	5	Matching five descriptions of people to eight short texts.
3	True / False Scanning for specific information.	10	Ten items with an adapted-authentic long text.
4	Four-option multiple choice Reading for detailed comprehension; understanding attitude, opinion and writer purpose. Reading for gist, inference and global meaning.	5	Long text.
5	Four-option multiple choice cloze Understanding of vocabulary and grammar in a short text. Reading for general and detailed meaning.	10	Factual or narrative text.

Writing

Part	Task Type and Focus	No. of items	Task Format
1	Sentence transformations Rephrasing and reformulating information.	5	Rewriting theme-related sentences where the beginning and end are supplied.
2	Short communicative message of 35–45 words.	1	A short message including three specific pieces of information in the form of a postcard, note, e-mail, etc.
3	A piece of continuous writing of about 100 words.	1	An informal letter or a story.

Paper 2 Listening

Part	Task Type and Focus	No. of items	Task Format
1	Three-option multiple choice Identifying key information from short exchanges.	7	Short monologues or dialogues with visuals.
2	Three-option multiple choice Identifying specific information and detailed meaning.	6	Longer monologue or interview (with one main speaker).
3	Gap-fill Identifying, understanding and interpreting information to fill gaps on a form or to complete notes.	6	Longer monologue of neutral or informal nature.
4	True / False Listening for detailed meaning, and to identify the attitudes and opinions of the speakers.	6	Longer informal dialogue.

Paper 3 Speaking

Part	Task Type and Focus	No. of items	Task Format
1	Each candidate interacts with the interlocutor.	2–3 minutes	Questions about personal information.
2	Candidates interact with each other. Making and responding to suggestions, discussing alternatives, making recommendations and negotiating agreement.	2-3 minutes	Simulated situation based on a visual stimulus.
3	Extended turn Responding to photographs and managing discourse in a longer turn.	3 minutes	Candidates talk for up to a minute each about one photo each on a related topic.
4	General conversation Candidates talk about their likes/dislikes, preferences, experiences, habits, etc.	3 minutes	Extended discussion on the topic of Part 3.

3

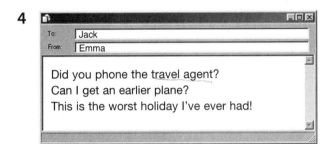

The hotel dining room is available for private parties on Sundays.

A   You cannot eat here at weekends.

B   Hotel guests can have parties in their rooms.

C   It is possible to hire the dining room.

4

| To: | Jack |
| From: | Emma |

Did you phone the travel agent?
Can I get an earlier plane?
This is the worst holiday I've ever had!

What does Emma want Jack to do?

A   arrange another holiday

B   fly out to meet her

C   find out about flight times

5

NOTICE
Discount Day next Friday!

Hundreds of our most popular products will be reduced for one day only! Don't miss it!

A   Everything in this shop will be cheaper on Friday.

B   There will be a discount on many items on Friday.

C   The shop's most popular products will cost less after Friday.

Part 2

Questions 6–10

The people below are all planning an evening's entertainment.
On the opposite page there are descriptions of eight evenings out.
Decide which evening would be the most suitable for the following people.
For questions **6–10**, mark the correct letter (**A–H**) on your answer sheet.

Tip ────────
Read the instructions carefully before you start. They will help you understand the task.

---

6  Anna is meeting an old school friend on Saturday night. She'd like to go somewhere they can chat and have a good meal, but hear some music at the same time.

7  Henri wants to listen to music in a lively place. He's a confident person and is going out alone in order to meet new people.

8  George is planning to celebrate the end of his exams with his friends on Friday night. They want music and dancing, but no food, as they don't have a lot of money.

9  Maria loves all kinds of music and wants to relax after a hard week at work. She'd like to sit quietly and listen to some music.

10  Carol is taking a colleague out. She's looking for a quiet place where they can eat and discuss some important plans for the future of their company.

EVENINGS OUT

A ***Julius Caesar* at the *Octagon***

A very modern and exciting performance of one of Shakespeare's most popular works! After great success in other parts of Europe this entertaining play comes to Britain for the first time.

B **70's Night!**

Party! Party! Party! There's no time to stop! DJ Mike Murray and his 70's disco music will keep you entertained all night! Eight until late this Friday. Light snacks available at the bar – if you've time!

C **Riverstone Restaurant**

We are proud to announce a new chef and a new menu at the Riverstone! Choose from a wide selection of modern European dishes. Restaurant opens 7 p.m. every evening. Live music every Friday and Saturday night after 9 p.m.

D **Hollywood Stars**

Make new friends and have fun at our Hollywood Stars night this weekend. Dress up as your favourite film star and enjoy a live band and disco.

E **Jazz and Stuff**

Jazz and Stuff is one of the best concerts this town has seen for ages. Stars from around the world entertain with jazz, blues, country, soul, rock 'n' roll and pop. There's something for everyone.

F **Life After Children**

A warm and entertaining play about a mother who is trying to look after her child and keep her job at the same time. This comedy should be seen by anyone with children – or anyone who's ever been a child!

G **Upton Hotel and Restaurant**

Set on the edge of town and in pretty gardens, the Upton Hotel is the perfect place for romantic evenings, business meetings or for talking to friends. The quiet and pleasant hotel provides exciting and creative menus as well as a high standard of service.

H **A Night Out at *Squares***

Squares is a great new club that provides different kinds of entertainment through the week. Comedy nights are on Fridays and Saturdays and there's live music on Mondays and Wednesdays. The rest of the week is dance time. Food available at lunchtimes only.

Part 3

Questions 11–20

Look at the sentences below about a trip to the Andes in Peru.
Read the text on the opposite page to decide if each sentence is correct or incorrect.
If it is correct, mark **A** on your answer sheet.
If it is not correct, mark **B** on your answer sheet.

11 This tour of Peru begins in the capital city. *A*

12 There are organised trips in Cusco. *A*

13 All sporting activities must be booked before arrival. *B*

14 The train ride through the mountains is non-stop. *B*

15 You need to pay more for the train ride. *B*

16 There is a choice of hotel for the whole trip. *B*

17 There is a chance to go on a trip as soon as you arrive in Lima. *B*

18 There are opportunities to buy local goods in the mountains. *A*

19 The mountain trip includes a talk by musicians. *B*

20 There is time to do an activity on the final full day in Lima. *B*

Tip

Read statements 11–20 carefully before you read the text, and underline the most important words.

Exploring Peru

Our tour will introduce you to the most beautiful parts of Peru, starting with the capital of the country, Lima. Here you can visit some excellent museums and eat in world-famous restaurants. You will also visit the mountain city of Cusco, which is a magical place with a relaxed atmosphere, colourful markets and a lively nightlife.

5 There are opportunities for you to explore the city at leisure, or you can choose to go sightseeing with our excellent guides. There is also a chance to go hiking, mountain biking, white water rafting, horse riding, paragliding and hot-air ballooning. Our guides will help you choose and book any activity as soon as you arrive.

From Cusco, you can take a train ride through the mountains of the Andes. This is the high 10 point of your tour and we have carefully chosen a route that will allow you to visit local villages and eat in local restaurants. There is also a visit to the ancient city of Macchu Picchu. The full cost of this mountain trip is included in the price of the tour.

We offer two choices of hotel grades for most of your stay. The nights in the mountains are spent together in local hotels. All our hotels are of the highest quality.

15 Days 1–3 Mid-morning flight from London Heathrow to Lima. You will be met on arrival at Lima airport and taken to your hotel. Just enough time to eat and sleep, and the next day you can join a sightseeing trip and spend your time getting to know the capital.

Days 4–6 Take an early morning flight to Cusco and explore the magical city.

20 Days 7–9 Take an unforgettable train ride through the mountains. Stay in a village and see a typical Inca home. There are plenty of beautiful local cloths and pots for sale. Listen to a traditional Peruvian band, who will give you a demonstration and an explanation of the musical instruments of the Andes. Visit the 25   ancient city of Macchu Picchu.

Day 10   Return to Cusco for another day to explore the beautiful city. Perhaps try one of the adventure sports on offer.

Day 11   Take the morning flight to Lima. Visit 30   the famous Gold Museum.

Day 12   Return flight to London.

Part 4

Questions 21–25

Read the text and questions below.
For each question, mark the correct letter **A, B, C** or **D** on your
answer sheet.

Tip

Read the title and the text quickly once for a general idea, then read it again more slowly.

Exercise can be fun!

Exercise has become a huge part of our world. There are gyms everywhere, but if you're not keen on them, there are hundreds of exercise videos to choose from. Exercise is good for you. It makes you feel better, look better and can help you live longer.

But what happens if you are the kind of person who would do anything rather than spend five
5 minutes on an exercise bike, including cleaning the house, visiting a boring relative or watching a terrible TV programme? If you are that kind of person, you need a plan!

First of all decide when you are going to exercise. Choose three times a week, like me. Write EXERCISE in your diary, on your calendar, on the wall if necessary! Then make sure you do it. Don't do anything else. I never make other arrangements.

10 Next, vary what you do. I went to the same aerobics class for two years! No wonder I was bored! Now I use different machines at the gym, I often change my jogging route and I never do aerobics.

Make exercise fun and find an exercise you enjoy. Why not play a sport, or join a dance class? I recently started a modern dance class. It's great fun and I've met lots of new people, but as
15 soon as I get bored I'll find something else!

21 What is the writer's main aim in writing the text?

    A to describe different ways of keeping fit

    B to persuade people about the benefits of exercise

    C to talk about the exercise classes she goes to

    D to encourage people to take exercise

22 What does the writer say about herself?

    A She prefers to exercise at home.

    B She isn't keen on joining classes.

    C She likes to do different kinds of exercise.

    D She doesn't like watching TV.

23 What does the reader learn about the writer's habits?

   A   She exercises three times a week.

   B   She often exercises with friends.

   C   She does aerobics regularly.

   D   She runs the same route every day.

24 What does she say about her dance class?

   A   She sometimes finds it boring.

   B   She may not do it forever.

   C   She thinks some people are unfriendly.

   D   She prefers doing sport.

25 What would be another good title for the article?

A

> Exercise may be boring, but it's good for you.

B

> **Many people do too much exercise.**

C

> **Regular exercise is best.**

D

> Exercising once a week is better than nothing.

Part 5

Questions 26–35

Read the text below and choose the correct word for each space.
For each question, mark the correct letter **A, B, C** or **D** on your answer sheet.

Example:

0 **A** recognising   **B** recommending   **C** regarding   **D** reviewing

Answer: | 0 | A ▬ B ▭ C ▭ D ▭ |

Studying abroad

More and more young people are **(0)** .... the advantages of living in **(26)** ....
country and are deciding to study abroad. They realise it's the best way to learn
(27) .... the customs and the way of life of other people. Student exchanges give
teenagers the **(28)** .... to live somewhere **(29)** .... for a school year.
(30) .... they are living abroad, they will eat new food, experience new traditions and
learn the way people **(31)** .... own age live from day to day.

Students stay with carefully chosen host families and attend a **(32)** .... school.
(33) .... student on the exchange programme has **(34)** .... who directly supports
them the whole time they are abroad. To qualify as an exchange student, you **(35)** ....
be aged between 15 and 18 years and be good at a foreign language.

---

26 A separate   **B** another   **C** different   **D** new

27 A for   **B** about   **C** of   **D** by

28 A opportunity   **B** occasion   **C** reason   **D** cause

29 A else   **B** well   **C** too   **D** also

30 A Whether   **B** Although   **C** However   **D** While

31 A its   **B** her   **C** their   **D** our

32 A home   **B** local   **C** near   **D** close

33 A Many   **B** Every   **C** All   **D** Both

34 A anybody   **B** everyone   **C** anyone   **D** somebody

35 A must   **B** ought   **C** have   **D** need

Tip

Read the title and the text quickly
once for a general idea **before** you
look at the choices.

Writing
Part 1

Questions 1–5

Here are some sentences about learning a language.
For each question, complete the second sentence so that it means the same as the first.
Use no more than three words.
Write only the missing words on your answer sheet.
You may use this page for any rough work.

Example:

0 I enjoyed learning languages at school.

I used .... **learning languages at school.**

Answer: | 0 | *to enjoy* |

---

1 I went to France because I wanted to improve my French.

I wanted to improve my French .... **I went to France.**

2 I find speaking in a foreign language embarrassing.

I get .... **when speaking in a foreign language.**

3 I prefer speaking English to writing it.

I like speaking English .... **writing it.**

Tip

Remember you need to write no more than three words.

4 I was taught Italian by a very good teacher.

The teacher .... **taught me Italian was very good.**

5 I'm better at languages than any other subject.

Languages are my .... **subject.**

Part 2

Question 6

You stayed with your English friend, Tom, last weekend.
Write an e-mail to Tom. In your e-mail, you should
- thank him for the visit
- say what you enjoyed most
- invite him to stay with you.

Write **35–45 words** on your answer sheet.

Tip

Read the instructions carefully and underline the most important words.

Part 3

Write an answer to **one** of the questions (**7** or **8**) in this part.
Write your answer in about **100 words** on your answer sheet.
Put the question number in the box at the top of your answer sheet.

Question 7

- Your English teacher has asked you to write a story.
- Your story must begin with this sentence.

> **When I opened the letter I found a plane ticket with my name on it.**

- Write your **story** on your answer sheet.

Tip

Remember to choose **only one** of the questions in this Part. Read them both carefully and underline the most important words. Decide which one you can do best, but don't spend too long deciding.

Question 8

- This is part of a letter you receive from your English friend, Mary.

> In your next letter, please tell me all about the party you went to last weekend. Did you enjoy it? Did you meet anybody interesting?

- Now write a letter to Mary answering her questions.
- Write your **letter** on your answer sheet.

Paper 2 Listening (about 30 minutes)
Part 1

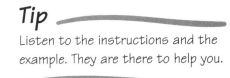

Questions 1–7

There are seven questions in this part.
For each question there are three pictures and a short recording.
Choose the correct picture and put a tick (✔) in the box below it.

Example: How does the woman travel to work?

A ☐   B ✔   C ☐

1 Who did the man see yesterday?

A ☐   B ☐   C ☐

2 Where's the computer?

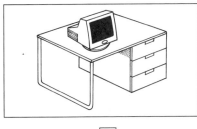 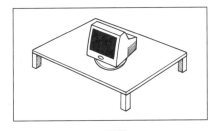 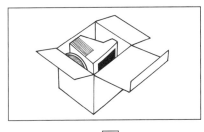

A ☐   B ☐   C ☐

3 What did the man have in the restaurant?

A ☐   B ☐   C ☐

4 What was stolen on Saturday?

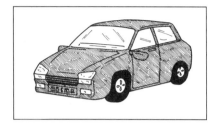  

A ☐ B ☐ C ☐

5 What does the man do?

A ☐ B ☐ C ☐

6 What time are they meeting?

A ☐ B ☐ C ☐

7 What is the weather like today?

 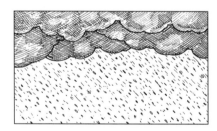 

A ☐ B ☐ C ☐

Part 2

Questions 8–13

You will hear someone welcoming a group of visitors to *Ocean Life* sea park.

For each question, put a tick (✔) in the correct box.

Tip

Use the time allowed to read the instructions and the questions quickly for an idea of what you will hear.

8 This group of visitors

- A have just arrived at the sea park. ☐
- B have finished their visit. ☐
- C have already seen some of *Ocean Life*. ☐

9 Visitors are encouraged to

- A see only the sea life they like best. ☐
- B take plenty of time to see everything. ☐
- C come back to the park for another visit. ☐

10 Organisers at the centre believe that

- A some sea life is more interesting than others. ☐
- B sharks should never be kept in a sea park. ☐
- C certain sea life should remain in the sea. ☐

11 What does the speaker say about learning at the sea park?

- A It's less important than being entertained. ☐
- B You can both learn and have fun. ☐
- C There is written information everywhere. ☐

12 How do the organisers make school visits easier?

- A They speak to teachers after the visits. ☐
- B They organise special school days. ☐
- C They make suggestions about what to study. ☐

13 The organisers also help sea life by

- A caring for hurt animals until they are well. ☐
- B looking after injured animals from all over the world. ☐
- C sending rescuers to look for animals in Europe. ☐

Part 3

Questions 14–19

You will hear somebody talking about a short break in Barcelona.
For each question, fill in the missing information in the numbered space.

Tip _____

Read the instructions and the
notes quickly for a general idea of
what kind of information is missing.
_____

SHORT BREAKS IN THE CITY

Length of City Breaks

From **(14)** .... to seven nights

Cost of Barcelona Break

Price includes **(15)** .... and bed and breakfast (not evening meals)

(pay less if you stay on a **(16)** .... night)

Extras

Pay more for a **(17)** .... card (allows money off city sights and some

(18) ....)

Travel Dates

5th – 31st **(19)** ....

Part 4

Questions 20–25

Look at the six sentences for this part.
You will hear a conversation between a girl, Anna, and a boy, James, about a party.
Decide if each sentence is correct or incorrect.
If it is correct, put a tick (✔) in the box under **A** for **YES**. If it is not correct, put a tick (✔) in the box under **B** for **NO**.

Tip

Read the instructions and the questions quickly for an idea of who will be talking about what.

		A	B
		YES	NO
20	James is looking forward to his brother's engagement.	☐	☐
21	James thinks his brother's girlfriend is boring.	☐	☐
22	Anna enjoys her family parties.	☐	☐
23	James gets on well with his cousins.	☐	☐
24	Anna reminds James to buy them a gift.	☐	☐
25	Both Anna and James have bought things on the internet before.	☐	☐

Paper 3 Speaking (10–12 minutes)

Part 1 Personal information (2–3 minutes)

Answer these questions:
What's your name?
What's your surname? How do you spell it?
Where do you live?
Do you work or are you a student?
Do you enjoy studying English?
Do you think that English will be useful to you in the future?
What do you enjoy doing in your free time?

Tip

Be ready to talk about yourself –
your personal details, what you do
every day, things you like doing, etc.

Part 2 Simulated situation (2–3 minutes)

You are choosing a present for your friend's wedding.
Look at the picture on page 21.
Talk about what presents you can buy, then decide which one to get.

Tip

Listen to the examiner's
instructions carefully. If you do not
understand, ask the examiner to
explain again.

Part 3 Responding to a photograph (3 minutes)

Candidate A: look at Photo 1 on page 94, show it to Candidate B
and talk about it.
Candidate B: look at Photo 2 on page 95, show it to Candidate A
and talk about it.

Tip

Look carefully at the photo, listen to
the examiner's instructions, and
think of some things to say **before**
you start speaking.

Part 4 General conversation based on the photographs (3 minutes)

Talk to each other about the kinds of transport you use. Talk about
what you like and dislike about different forms of transport.

Tip

The conversation will be connected to
the photos, so you can use some of
the ideas you talked about in Part 3.

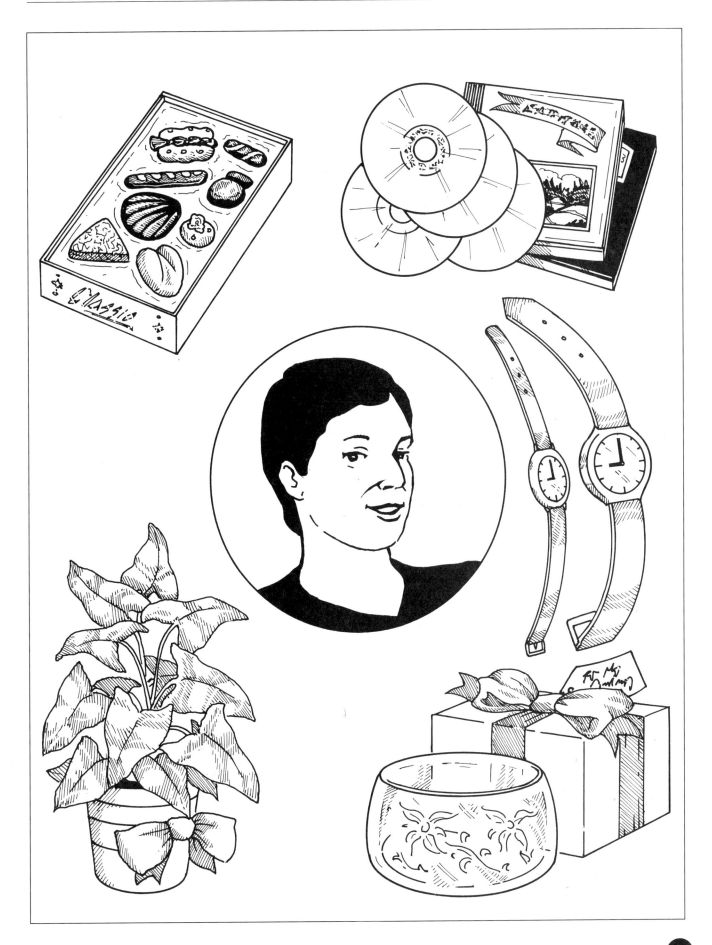

Test 2

Paper 1 Reading and Writing (1 hour 30 minutes)

Reading
Part 1

Tip
Read each sign carefully. Think 'Why is it here?', 'Who is it for?', 'Where would I see it?'

Questions 1–5

Look at the text in each question.
What does it say?
Mark the correct letter **A**, **B** or **C** on your answer sheet.

Example:

0

> **Use these doors only
> in an emergency.**

A You must never leave by these doors.

B The doors can be used if necessary.

C Only some people can use these doors.

Answer: 0 | A B C

1

> **The gym is closed
> 3–5 p.m. Friday for
> staff training.**

A The public can use the gym for part of Friday.

B The gym is closed for one day.

C No staff are available on Friday after 5 p.m.

2

> **Take one tablet twice
> a day with food.**

A You should eat before you take these tablets.

B You should take these tablets for two days.

C You should have two tablets per day.

3

NOTICE

LOST BOOK

If anyone finds my English book, please hand it in at the lost property office — I left it in the library yesterday.

Juan García-Lopez

What does Juan want people to do?

A   return his property to the library

B   look for his lost English book

C   give him back his library book

4

MESSAGE

To: Tom
From: Joe

Tom – Football training is cancelled until further notice because Mike has gone away, maybe we could do something else this week.

Tom and Joe aren't playing football because

A   they're going away for a week.

B   Mike is somewhere else.

C   training is on another day.

5

No dogs allowed anywhere on the beach between May and September.

A   Dog owners must avoid certain areas of the beach.

B   You can never take your dog onto this beach.

C   Dogs are welcome at certain times of the year.

Part 2

Questions 6–10

The people below are choosing a video to hire for the evening.
On the opposite page there are descriptions of eight videos.
Decide which video would be the most suitable for the following people.
For questions **6–10**, mark the correct letter (**A–H**) on your answer sheet.

6

Sarah enjoys <u>watching films</u> that scare her, if they are well made. She doesn't like to be able to guess what's going to happen.

> ***Tip***
>
> Don't start answering the questions until you have read **all** the information at least once.

7

Maria prefers serious films that are about people and relationships. She likes watching stories that take place in the past.

8

Simon has a stressful job and relaxes by watching fun films that entertain him and are easy to understand. He likes to laugh and he likes to <u>guess what's going to happen</u>!

9

Juan likes films that make him think, but doesn't like to be scared. He's also keen on history and sport.

10

Sally enjoys well made and <u>serious crime stories</u>. She likes films that surprise her but isn't keen on love stories.

BEST OF THE VIDEOS

A **Going Home**

When Marco returns to his home village in South America after two years away, he hopes to find his girlfriend waiting for him. Instead, he discovers she has been kidnapped. An old story with some new ideas and a shock ending! Don't miss it!

B **The Lost Gold**

In the middle of the desert, a group of people are searching for lost gold. When they find it, however, they also discover a terrible 3,000-year old secret! This frightening film is non-stop action with excellent acting and a clever story. You'll never guess the ending! But be warned – don't watch this film with the lights out!

C **Worst Wishes**

When Marcie wishes that the nasty girls at school would disappear, her wish comes true! She makes another wish and then another. Soon Marcie is controlling her school, her family and her town! This would be frightening if it wasn't so easy to guess the story!

D **Lonely Lives**

When ex-footballer Jack Powell returns home for a friend's wedding, the memories of his thirteenth birthday come rushing back. Most of the film happens in the 1960s and it's about a lonely boy who becomes friends with a lonely man. There are no surprises in the film, but it's well made and entertaining.

E **Perfect Couple**

Two people are pushed into a dangerous high-speed adventure when they find a suitcase full of money. They leave town and try to start a new life but somebody else has different ideas! This is a love story with a difference that may disturb you!

F **My Father**

Sam wants to play baseball, like his father before him. He's the best player in his school, so why isn't he picked for the team? Sam soon finds out that it's his father who is stopping him from playing. What he wants to find out is why! This excellent story will keep you guessing to the end.

G **The Search**

What do a teacher, an ex-criminal, a policeman and a dentist have in common? They're all searching for a million dollars in cash! The only question is – who's going to get it? A simple story with fast action and great comedy!

H **Arrival of a stranger**

Amy lives in a quiet town where nothing happens. But when a stranger comes to town people suddenly start to disappear. A fast-moving comedy set in the 1970's, with a surprise ending!

Part 3

Questions 11–20

Look at the sentences below about doing courses on the internet.
Read the text on the opposite page to decide if each sentence is correct or incorrect.
If it is correct, mark **A** on your answer sheet.
If it is not correct, mark **B** on your answer sheet.

11 Most people do more than one course with Learn Now.

12 Learn Now is only for people who have done well at school.

13 With Learn Now, people study only the subjects they feel
are necessary.

14 Testing is an important part of Learn Now.

15 Some companies use Learn Now for training their employees.

16 You must have some basic skills to be able to do a computing course.

17 Learn Now recommends all students learn at a centre.

18 You can begin learning as soon as you contact Learn Now.

19 Learning at a centre means attending regularly.

20 Everybody must go to a centre for training at least once.

Tip ———
Read the title and the text quickly
for a general idea then read it again
more slowly.

Learn Now

Learning is for life

People who begin Learn Now soon find that
learning is fun and that it doesn't have to
stop at school or at college. It's something
5 you can do all your life. Over half those
taking Learn Now courses come back and
study again and again.

What is Learn Now?

Learn Now is perfect for anyone who hasn't
10 been successful with traditional ways of learning and wants to try something different. The courses
allow you to learn just what you want to learn when you want to learn it. You don't have to do a
long course that may include many things that you don't actually need. And you don't have to
take any exams!

Who is Learn Now for?

15 Everyone can benefit from Learn Now – from company employees who need to learn new skills
quickly, to people wanting to return to work. Many businesses use Learn Now as part of their staff
development. Others have found that an extra skill has helped them to change their career paths
while many people use Learn Now just for their own interest.

What courses can I do?

20 There are over 400 courses to choose from, so there is something for everyone. The most popular
courses are in computing and you can do any of these at any stage. Business courses are also
very popular and there are some excellent 'Skills for Life' courses that help you improve your
maths and communication skills. Remember you don't need experience or knowledge for any of
our courses.

Where do I learn with Learn Now?

25
You can learn by distance learning at home or at work, or you can go to one of our Learning
Centres. However, if you are very new to the world of the internet and computing, we do suggest
you come to a centre where we can guide you along in person.

How do I get started?

30 Just call in or telephone one of our centres and we will get you started without delay. If you want
to learn at one of our learning centres, we will ask you to come in for some training, and from
then on you just book in whenever you want to. If you want to work only at home, or at the office,
we can organise everything by telephone or e-mail. We'll start you off with some basic training
and then keep in contact with you to make sure you are getting the best from Learn Now. Our
35 skilled staff are always available to help.

Part 4

Questions 21–25

Read the text and questions below.
For each question, mark the correct letter **A, B, C** or **D** on your answer sheet.

Night Work

Can you imagine what it would be like working at night? You'd start your day when everyone else was going to bed, and you'd go to bed when everyone else was getting up. Is that really a natural way to live?

5 These days more and more jobs need to be done at night. Most big hotels offer 24-hour room service, and need staff at reception and working in the bars. Many companies have 24-hour call centres to deal with emergency enquiries. There are 24-hour supermarkets, and of course there are the workers for the emergency services such as fire-fighters, the police and hospital workers.

However, few people can work well at night. This is partly because we cannot easily change our sleeping habits. Some people can manage on as little as three hours' sleep while
10 others need as many as eleven hours – you're either a 'short sleeper' or a 'long sleeper'. If working at night stops you from getting the amount of sleep you need, you will damage your health.

The best part of the day for everyone is around lunchtime and the worst point is between 2 a.m. and 4 a.m. So if you're driving home at this time or doing
15 something important at work, things are far more likely to go wrong!

Humans are used to sleeping at night and being awake during the day, and they'll never be able to do things the other way round. The problem is that today's 24-hour society isn't going to slow down which means that night-workers will remain.

21 What is the writer's main aim in writing the text?

A to describe the importance of work

B to say how working at night can be bad for you

C to suggest how people can change their way of life

D to recommend people spend more time sleeping

Tip
Remember that for some questions you need to understand the **whole** meaning of the text. You may need to look in different parts of the text for the answer.

22 What does the writer say about night jobs?

    A   Many people <u>refuse</u> to work at night.

    B   It is easier than working during the day.

    C   It is easier to demand better working conditions.

    D   There is a variety of them.

23 What would a reader learn about sleep from the text?

    A   Everybody needs the same amount.

    B   It's difficult to change your sleeping needs.

    C   People sleep better in the early morning.

    D   Many people need more than 11 hours' sleep.

24 What does the writer say about the future?

    A   Fewer people will work during the day.

    B   Some jobs will always be done at night.

    C   People will demand fewer services.

    D   People will work longer hours.

25 Which of the following could also be a title for this text?

A
> **A good night's sleep can change your life!**

B
> **A worker that sleeps more, works more!**

C
> **Society is changing but our bodies are not!**

D
> **The loneliest jobs in the world!**

Part 5

Questions 26–35

Read the text below and choose the correct word for each space.
For each question, mark the correct letter **A, B, C** or **D** on your answer sheet.

Example:

0 A much   **B** further   **C** away   **D** far

Answer: 0 | A | B | C | D

Good walks

You're rarely **(0)**................... from a good walk in Britain – **(26)**................... you live in the town or the country. From mountains in the North to gentle hills in the South, you're **(27)**................... to find some wide open spaces you will like. People **(28)**................... live in the city can enjoy walks **(29)**................... canals and in the many beautiful parks to be found.

Walking gives you the **(30)**................... of exercise and at the same time allows you to experience wonderful scenery. You can also **(31)**................... about local wildlife. On foot, in the countryside, you see much more than you'd **(32)**................... see from a car or on a bike.

However, if you are out and about in the countryside make sure you follow the rules. You mustn't go **(33)**................... that's private, you **(34)**................... stay on public footpaths and **(35)**................... animals in fields!

26 **A** whether   **B** while   **C** because   **D** although

27 **A** confident **B** sure   **C** definite   **D** clear

28 **A** who   **B** whom   **C** whose   **D** which

29 **A** round   **B** through   **C** along   **D** between

30 **A** help   **B** benefit   **C** assistance **D** allowance

31 **A** know   **B** find   **C** learn   **D** look

32 **A** ever   **B** never   **C** yet   **D** always

33 **A** any   **B** anywhere   **C** anyway   **D** anyhow

34 **A** could   **B** ought   **C** would   **D** should

35 **A** stay   **B** avoid   **C** keep   **D** let

Tip

Read the text a second time more slowly. Read each complete sentence not each line.

Writing
Part 1

Questions 1–5

Here are some sentences about food.
For each question, complete the second sentence so that it means the same as the first.
Use no more than three words.
Write only the missing words on your answer sheet.
You may use this page for any rough work.

Example:

0 My parents asked me if I was eating well.

My parents said to me, '..................... **well?'**

Answer: | 0 | *Are you eating* |

---

1 Fish is better for you than meat.

Meat isn't .... **for you as fish.**

2 Snacks can be bought in the café.

You .... **in the café.**

Tip ─────────
Look at the words before and after
the gap to help with the meaning.
─────────

3 He can cook really well.

He's really .... **cooking.**

4 There are only a few good restaurants in this area.

There aren't very .... **good restaurants in this area.**

5 It is a good idea to eat plenty of fruit and vegetables.

Everybody .... **plenty of fruit and vegetables.**

Part 2

Question 6

You forgot your friend Paul's birthday.
Write a note to Paul. In your note, you should
- apologise for forgetting his birthday
- suggest you take him out for a meal
- say when you are free.

Write **35–45 words** on your answer sheet.

Tip

Look at the verbs like *thank, suggest, tell, offer, invite,* etc. Don't just repeat these verbs in your answer – think about what to write that has the meaning of these verbs.

Part 3

Write an answer to **one** of the questions (**7** or **8**) in this part.
Write your answer in about **100 words** on your answer sheet.
Put the question number in the box at the top of your answer sheet.

Question 7

- Your English teacher has asked you to write a story.
- Your story must begin with this sentence:

  ### I was surprised when I arrived at the bus stop.

- Write your **story** on your answer sheet.

Tip

Plan your ideas before you start. Think of the best order to put them in.

Question 8

- This is part of a letter you receive from your English penfriend, Jane.

> I really like basketball. What's your favourite sport?

- Now write a letter to Jane, telling her about your favourite sport.
- Write your **letter** on your answer sheet.

Tip

Begin 'Dear ...' and write a suitable ending, e.g. 'Love from ...'.

Paper 2 Listening (about 30 minutes)
Part 1

Questions 1–7

There are seven questions in this part.
For each question there are three pictures and a short recording.
Choose the correct picture and put a tick (✔) in the box below it.

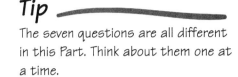
Tip
The seven questions are all different in this Part. Think about them one at a time.

Example: How does the woman travel to work?

A ☐   B ✔   C ☐

---

1 How did the accident happen?

A ☐   B ☐   C ☐

2 What pet are they going to buy?

A ☐   B ☐   C ☐

3 Where is the mobile phone?

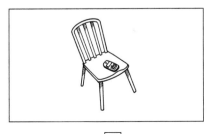 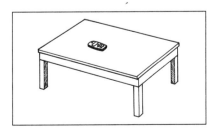 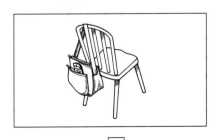

A ☐   B ☐   C ☐

4 When are they going to celebrate the end of their exams?

A ☐   B ☐   C ☐

5 What does Alison's new boyfriend look like?

A ☐   B ☐   C ☐

6 Where has Sally been?

A ☐   B ☐   C ☐

7 What can you buy during the interval?

A ☐   B ☐   C ☐

Part 2

Questions 8–13

You will hear someone reviewing a music night.
For each question, put a tick (✔) in the correct box.

8 The Old Oak is going to

A stop serving food. ☐
B introduce music at lunchtimes. ☐
C try to attract different kinds of people. ☐

9 Bands who play at the Old Oak

A will play for nothing. ☐
B can play in the pub before they perform. ☐
C have to book three weeks before. ☐

10 *Living World* have

A recently formed. ☐
B just moved to the area. ☐
C changed their sound. ☐

11 What happened during part of the band's performance?

A There was a problem with some equipment. ☐
B They stopped playing for a while. ☐
C Somebody was injured. ☐

12 The pub was quite empty because

A many of the band's fans were away. ☐
B only local people knew about the performance. ☐
C a lot of people left early. ☐

13 What must bands do if they want to play at the pub?

A prove all their members are locals ☐
B send an example of their music ☐
C show they have had previous success ☐

Part 3

Questions 14–19

You will hear somebody on the radio talking about a restaurant.
For each question, fill in the missing information in the
numbered space.

Tip _____

If a word is spelt out on the
recording, your spelling **must** be
correct.
_____

The Rooftop Restaurant

Address: Market Street,

(14) .... Village

Opening day: **(15)** .... 18th October

Lunch time

Opening times: **(16)** .... a.m. – 3 p.m.

Menu: Two-course menu

(pay extra for **(17)** ....)

Evening

Opening times: 7 p.m. – 10 p.m.

Menu: Three-course menu

(free **(18)** .... until 31st Oct)

Group bookings

Contact us **(19)** .... weeks before event

Part 4

Questions 20–25

Tip
Remember that you will hear the answers to the questions in order.

Look at the six sentences for this part.
You will hear a conversation between a girl, Meg, and a boy, David, about their plans for the future.
Decide if each sentence is correct or incorrect.
If it is correct, put a tick (✔) in the box under **A** for **YES**. If it is not correct, put a tick (✔) in the box under **B** for **NO**.

	A	B
	YES	NO
20 David immediately advises Meg not to take a year off.	☐	☐
21 Meg plans to get a well-paid job during her year off.	☐	☐
22 Meg feels going abroad will benefit her studies.	☐	☐
23 Meg and David agree that you can get life experience at home.	☐	☐
24 Meg is used to travelling.	☐	☐
25 Meg decides to go travelling after her course instead.	☐	☐

Paper 3 Speaking (10–12 minutes)

Part 1 Personal information (2–3 minutes)

Answer these questions:
What's your name?
What's your surname? How do you spell it?
Where do you live?
Do you work or are you a student?
Do you enjoy studying English?
Do you think that English will be useful to you in the future?
What do you enjoy doing in your free time?

Tip

Think about the right tense to use when talking about yourself, e.g. 'I live/work/like/have', 'Yesterday I went'.

Part 2 Simulated situation (2–3 minutes)

You are planning a weekend at a camp-site.
Look at the picture on page 39.
Talk together about the different places to camp and then decide on the best one.

Tip

Look at the pictures before you start speaking and think of some things you can say.

Part 3 Responding to a photograph (3 minutes)

Candidate A: look at Photo 1 on page 96, show it to Candidate B and talk about it.
Candidate B: look at Photo 2 on page 97, show it to Candidate A and talk about it.

Tip

Don't worry if you don't know the right word for something in the photo. If you need to talk about it, use a word with a similar meaning, or explain what you mean.

Part 4 General conversation based on the photographs (3 minutes)

Talk to each other about what you do at the weekend. Talk about your favourite kinds of entertainment.

Tip

Listen carefully to the examiner's instructions. Ask if you aren't sure what to do.

Test 3

Paper 1 Reading and Writing (1 hour 30 minutes)

Reading
Part 1

Questions 1–5

Look at the text in each question.
What does it say?
Mark the correct letter **A**, **B** or **C** on your answer sheet.

Example:

0

Use these doors only
in an emergency.

A You must never leave by these doors.

B The doors can be used if necessary.

C Only some people can use these doors.

Tip

Don't choose the first option you think is right. Look carefully at the meaning of each option before you decide.

Answer: | 0 | A ── B ▬ C ── |

1

There is no longer
a delivery charge
on orders of pizza.

A This restaurant gives a free pizza with every order.

B You don't have to pay for a pizza delivery.

C Some orders of pizza cannot be delivered.

2

Passengers without passes
should have the correct
fare. Drivers are unable to
give change.

A Passengers must have a pass or the exact money.

B Some fares on this bus route have changed.

C You can only travel on this bus if you have a pass.

3

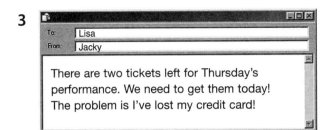

To: Lisa
From: Jacky

There are two tickets left for Thursday's performance. We need to get them today! The problem is I've lost my credit card!

What does Jacky want Lisa to do?

A   cancel an arrangement

B   find her credit card

C   buy some tickets

4

Please wait here until a member of staff takes you to your seat.

A   Somebody will show you where you can sit.

B   If you don't want to wait you can go straight to your seat.

C   You should go to your seat and wait for a member of staff.

5

Notice

Friday's concert is cancelled. Anybody who has bought a ticket should come to my office today and their money will be returned.

Simon Anderson

A   Tickets for the concert can be bought from Simon's office.

B   There are no tickets left for Friday's concert.

C   You can have your money back if you have bought a ticket.

Part 2

Questions 6–10

The people below are planning to stay in a hotel in Paris.
On the opposite page there are descriptions of eight hotels.
Decide which hotel would be the most suitable for the following people.
For questions **6–10**, mark the correct letter (**A–H**) on your answer sheet.

---

6  Maria is a student planning to meet some friends for the weekend. She'd like to stay in the centre so that they can easily get to bars and clubs. She doesn't want to spend much on food.

Tip ———

Underline the key words in descriptions 6–10.

7  Stefan is going on a business trip and wants to stay in a hotel where he can hire a room for meetings. He'd like to eat at the hotel and be able to get to and from the airport easily.

8  Eleni has a stressful job and would like to spend a weekend shopping. She'd like to stay in a hotel which is close to the shops and which offers plenty of leisure facilities.

9  Kathryn and Klaus would like to stay in a quiet part of Paris. They are keen to explore the sights, but would prefer the hotel to organise trips.

10  Paolo would like to spend time studying French painting. He's travelling alone so would prefer to stay in a hotel where he'll have the chance to meet other people.

PARIS HOTELS

A   **Hotel Inn**

The Hotel Inn is a large and modern hotel in the centre of Paris. The nearest Metro station is only 100 metres away, which makes it easy to reach the main train station and the airport. As well as TV, telephone and mini-bar, there is a choice of three restaurants, and facilities for conferences.

B   **La Villette**

La Villette is a large hotel close to the waters of the Canal St Martin. The science museum, with its displays of the latest in scientific technology, is also nearby. Breakfast only is included.

C   **The Trocadero**

The Trocadero is a traditional hotel with a very friendly atmosphere in a popular part of Paris. It is perfect for art lovers, being close to many of Paris' most famous galleries. There is also a bar where guests can socialise in the evenings.

D   **Hotel Etoile**

The Hotel Etoile is within walking distance of the best stores in Paris. The Hotel has a heated swimming pool, steam room and gym. All meals are included.

E   **La Villa**

La Villa is a reasonably priced hotel in a very fashionable and central part of Paris, amongst antique shops, cafés, and lively streets. It is the perfect place for those wishing to enjoy Paris nightlife. La Villa has an excellent restaurant, and all meals are included in the price.

F   **The Comfort Inn**

The Comfort Inn is between the centre of Paris and Disneyland Paris. All rooms have TV with free movies, and for the more active, there is a golf course a few minutes' walk away. Breakfast is provided daily, and lunch and dinner from Monday to Thursday. Free car parking is available.

G   **Hotel Bel Air**

The hotel is in a peaceful part of Paris away from the main tourist attractions, although the hotel will arrange group sightseeing. There are pleasant gardens and an excellent restaurant.

H   **Hotel Petite**

The Hotel Petite is a busy family-run hotel not far from the main train station. It provides buffet breakfast, and is close to many excellent restaurants for other meals.

Part 3

Questions 11–20

Look at the sentences below about a centre that teaches music.
Read the text on the opposite page to decide if each sentence is correct or incorrect.
If it is correct, mark **A** on your answer sheet.
If it is not correct, mark **B** on your answer sheet.

---

11 Advice is offered to new pupils on special open days.

12 The maximum number of pupils learning an instrument in a small group is four.

13 Beginners can be taught their instrument on their own.

14 All lessons take place at the same school.

Tip ───────

Remember that questions 11–20 are in the order of the text.

───────

15 It is possible to have a lesson at the weekend.

16 Parents should buy an instrument as soon as they apply for a place.

17 Singing helps students to improve other skills.

18 Singers are expected to take exams.

19 Only eight children can attend a 'Musical Youth' class at the same time.

20 Parents can join in the 'Musical Youth' classes.

Music for Life

Learning music is important for the educational and personal development of young people! Learning music is also great fun!

Learning an Instrument: how do pupils choose?

All our teachers are highly qualified and experienced musicians, and pupils can learn to play a wide range of instruments, from the keyboard to the drums. We have open days when new pupils who are unsure which instrument to choose can come to the centre. They are able to speak to teachers about which instrument might be best for them, and they can also see and hear classes in action.

How are pupils taught?

Pupils can learn in small groups, in classes or individually, depending on their needs. Small groups of three or four pupils have lessons that last for a minimum of thirty minutes. Class lessons last for a minimum of forty-five minutes and have at least ten pupils. Individual lessons are offered only to pupils who have some experience.

When and where do lessons take place?

Lessons are available in many schools, usually during the day. If there is no lesson available for a particular instrument in a particular school, other arrangements can be made at one of our music centres for lessons on Saturday afternoons or weekday evenings.

Who is responsible for buying the instruments?

Parents usually have to provide instruments and music. But parents of beginners are advised not to buy an instrument until they are told that a place is available. They should also find out from the teacher the most suitable type of instrument to get.

Singing lessons: what are the benefits?

The Centre also offers singing lessons. Singing can encourage young people to develop different abilities. It can help with communication, and for those who go to drama school, singing provides good training for acting too. Pupils can come for an hour every week to sing and just enjoy themselves, or they can choose to take exams and sing at concerts.

Starting young: when can pupils begin?

Children are never too young to become interested in music. We have special 'Musical Youth' classes for children from the age of 3½ to 8. These are designed to encourage young children to enjoy music through a variety of activities including singing, musical games, listening and movement. 'Musical Youth' classes take place on Saturday mornings with groups of about 18 children. A parent or other adult must attend each session, and they are encouraged to sit with their child and help them with the activities.

Part 4

Questions 21–25

Read the text and questions below.
For each question, mark the correct letter **A, B, C** or **D** on your answer sheet.

A healthy mind

The brain is the most amazing part of our body and despite all medical research nobody really understands everything about it. But just like our bodies, it needs to be cared for in ways that can be quite simple. Getting a good night's sleep, eating a balanced diet and taking deep breaths are all important methods of looking after both your body and

5   your brain.

Many people think their brain will slow down with age and their memory will get worse as a result. The truth is, just like your body, you can also improve your mind. I've found I can improve my memory by imagining what I need to remember. For example, if I'm going shopping and I need bread, milk and a birthday card for my brother, I imagine a

10   loaf of bread, a carton of milk with a cow on the front and a birthday card with a football on it.

The same kind of method can be used with important dates. If you have a picture in your mind of a particular event it's much easier to remember than just a number on a calendar.

Another way of improving your mind is to make sure you regularly visit new places and

15   have new experiences. Personally I find learning Spanish is a great way to keep the brain working, but communication in any language is important. Having a conversation is so much better for your brain than staring at a computer screen or at other people talking on TV.

21 What is the writer's main aim in writing the text?

A   to explain how the brain works

B   to talk about problems with the brain

C   to describe how clever she has become

D   to suggest the brain needs attention

Tip _____

Read each question and choices one at a time and underline the most important words.

22 What does the reader learn about the writer from the text?

A   She has a computer.

B   She is learning another language.

C   She likes shopping.

D   She enjoys travelling.

23 What does the writer say about the brain?

A   It should be treated in a similar way to our bodies.

B   Not enough medical research is being done on it.

C   It definitely becomes less quick when we are older.

D   It ages faster than our bodies.

24 What does the writer say about her own memory?

A   It has been possible to make it better.

B   She finds objects more difficult to remember than numbers.

C   It has got worse over the years.

D   She often forgets birthdays.

25 What would be another title for the text?

A
Easy ways to develop your mind.

B
The latest research into the brain.

C
The amazing power of memory.

D
How to remember things you thought you'd forgotten.

Part 5

Questions 26–35

Read the text below and choose the correct word for each space.
For each question, mark the correct letter **A, B, C** or **D** on your answer sheet.

Example:

0 A much   **B** large   **C** many   **D** great

Answer: | 0 | A   B   C   D

Different sides of Egypt

When most people think of Egypt they think of ancient history, but in fact Egypt offers **(0)** ....*much*.... more. There are **(26)** .... many different Egypts to enjoy – it just depends **(27)** .... how you're feeling. On some days Egypt **(28)** .... a country of beautiful palaces and days spent visiting the pyramids at Giza. On others you have a **(29)** .... to find bargains in the lively markets of Old Cairo. Egypt also **(30)** .... adventure tours including visits to the desert, and sports including scuba diving and **(31)** .... golf and fishing. For people who just want to relax, they can lie in the sun **(32)** .... the sea, or go on a boat **(33)** .... down the River Nile, watching birds and crocodiles. In the evening they can visit fine restaurants and **(34)** .... time enjoying the exciting night life, or going out to the opera. Whoever you are, whatever you like doing, you'll find something you'll love **(35)** .... Egypt.

---

26 **A** too   **B** more   **C** over   **D** so

27 **A** in   **B** on   **C** from   **D** of

28 **A** means   **B** knows   **C** understands   **D** feels

29 **A** time   **B** possibility   **C** chance   **D** method

30 **A** goes   **B** does   **C** provides   **D** offers

31 **A** even   **B** still   **C** yet   **D** however

32 **A** along   **B** by   **C** through   **D** next

33 **A** tour   **B** trip   **C** visit   **D** break

34 **A** make   **B** find   **C** have   **D** spend

35 **A** at   **B** for   **C** about   **D** with

Tip

Before you look at the choices, think of a word which might fit. If it is one of the choices, it may be the right answer, but try all the other choices too before deciding.

Writing
Part 1

Questions 1–5

Here are some sentences about living abroad.
For each question, complete the second sentence so that it means the same as the first.
Use no more than three words.
Write only the missing words on your answer sheet.
You may use this page for any rough work.

Example:

0 When I was a child my family lived in Spain.

    My family used .... **in Spain when I was a child.**

Answer: | 0 | *to live* |

---

1 Living abroad is more exciting than going on holiday.

    Going on holiday isn't as .... **living abroad.**

Tip ━━━━━━━━

Look for structures you recognise in the first sentence. Underline them and think of a different way of writing the same thing.

2 If you want to work in some countries, you need to have a visa.

    You can't work in some countries .... **you have a visa.**

3 When I started living there, my German improved.

    My German improved as .... **I started living there.**

4 Travelling alone in a foreign country is difficult.

    It isn't .... **travelling alone in a foreign country.**

5 He's too young to work abroad.

    He isn't old .... **to work abroad.**

49

Part 2

Question 6

You are having a birthday party.
Write an e-mail to your English friend, Anna. In your e-mail, you should
- invite her to the party
- offer to pick her up from the station
- suggest she stays with you for a few days.

Write **35–45 words** on your answer sheet.

Tip
Make some notes before you start writing. Decide on the best order. It is probably the same as the order of the three points in the question.

Part 3

Write an answer to **one** of the questions (**7** or **8**) in this part.
Write your answer in about **100 words** on your answer sheet.
Put the question number in the box at the top of your answer sheet.

Question 7

- This is part of a letter you receive from your English penfriend.

> In your next letter, please tell me all about your weekends. Who do you spend time with? What do you like doing best?

- Now write a letter answering your friend's questions.
- Write your **letter** on your answer sheet.

Tip
Remember you must write about 100 words.

Question 8

- Your English teacher has asked you to write a story.
- Your story must have the following title:

The Rainy Day

- Write your **story** on your answer sheet.

Tip
Make sure you have a beginning, middle and end in your plan before you start writing.

Paper 2 Listening (about 30 minutes)
Part 1

Tip ═══

Look at the pictures and think about what is different about them before you hear the recording. ═══

Questions 1–7

There are seven questions in this part.
For each question there are three pictures and a short recording.
Choose the correct picture and put a tick (✔) in the box below it.

Example: How does the woman travel to work?

A ☐   B ✔   C ☐

---

1 What time will the train arrive at the station?

A ☐   B ☐   C ☐

2 What is the woman going to do on holiday?

A ☐   B ☐   C ☐

3 What is the guest going to talk about?

 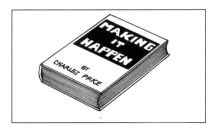 

A ☐   B ☐   C ☐

4 Where did the man go last night?

A ☐

B ☐

C ☐

5 Where does Anna live now?

A ☐

B ☐

C ☐

6 What does the man's teacher look like?

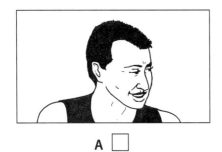
A ☐

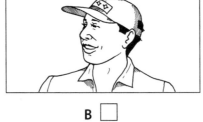
B ☐

C ☐

7 Where is the letter?

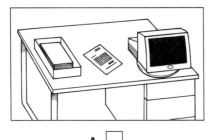
A ☐

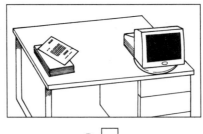
B ☐

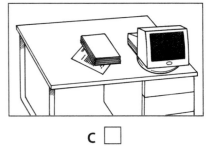
C ☐

Part 2

Questions 8–13

You will hear an interview with a writer.
For each question, put a tick (✔) in the correct box.

Tip ━━━━━
Don't decide too quickly. Some of the answers may be similar, and you may hear something about more than one of them.
━━━━━

8 Jack started writing when he

    A worked at a school. ☐

    B gave up his job as a teacher. ☐

    C was very young. ☐

9 Jack keeps fit by

    A exercising every day. ☐

    B running every morning. ☐

    C going for walks. ☐

10 Jack eats his lunch

    A at the same time every day. ☐

    B away from his computer. ☐

    C while he is writing. ☐

11 Jack likes to write

    A only in his office. ☐

    B in different places. ☐

    C in the kitchen. ☐

12 How long does it take Jack to completely finish a novel?

    A about six months ☐

    B more than a year ☐

    C less than twelve months ☐

13 What does Jack do after he's finished a novel?

    A He goes away on his own. ☐

    B He stops writing for a while. ☐

    C He starts writing something else. ☐

Part 3

Questions 14–19

You will hear somebody talking about a fashion show.
For each question, fill in the missing information in the numbered space.

Iffley College, Dublin – Fashion Show

The Date

(14) .... 25th June

The Place

Drama studio on the (15) ....
of the college

The Timetable

11.30 a.m.	Men's fashion (including (16) ....)
12.30 p.m.	Lunch (served in the (17) ....)
1.30 p.m.	Women's fashion (including summer and winter wear)
(18)	Presentation by fashion students at the college

Further information

Buy tickets over the phone, on the website
or at the college (19) ....

Information about the clothes can be found on the
college website or in your programme.

Part 4

Questions 20–25

Look at the six sentences for this part.
You will hear a conversation between a girl, Sarah, and a boy, Thomas, about moving abroad.
Decide if each sentence is correct or incorrect.
If it is correct, put a tick (✔) in the box under **A** for **YES**. If it is not correct, put a tick (✔) in the box under **B** for **NO**.

		A	B
		YES	NO
20	Thomas and Sarah agree that moving away is difficult.	☐	☐
21	Thomas thinks people will go and see Sarah.	☐	☐
22	Sarah's parents have bought a house in the south of Spain.	☐	☐
23	Sarah's parents have only recently thought about moving abroad.	☐	☐
24	The whole of Sarah's family are moving to Spain.	☐	☐
25	Sarah is confident about her ability to speak Spanish.	☐	☐

Tip

Think about the most important words in the questions. Listen for different ways of saying the same thing.

Paper 3 Speaking (10–12 minutes)

Part 1 Personal information (2–3 minutes)

Answer these questions:
What's your name?
What's your surname? How do you spell it?
Where do you live?
Do you work or are you a student?
Do you enjoy studying English?
Do you think that English will be useful to you in the future?
What do you enjoy doing in your free time?

Tip

Make sure you can spell words like your name and address. Make sure you know how to say the letters of the alphabet properly.

Part 2 Simulated situation (2–3 minutes)

You've decided you need to do more exercise.
Look at the picture on page 57.
Talk about what activities would be most enjoyable.

Tip

Remember that this is a discussion. Talk with your partner. Allow them to speak but make sure you talk too.

Part 3 Responding to a photograph (3 minutes)

Candidate A: look at Photo 1 on page 98, show it to Candidate B and talk about it.
Candidate B: look at Photo 2 on page 94, show it to Candidate A and talk about it.

Tip

Don't worry if you can't think of anything to say. The examiner will help you by asking questions.

Part 4 General conversation based on the photographs (3 minutes)

Talk to each other about where you live. Talk about what you like and dislike about your area.

Tip

Remember to talk to your partner, not the examiner. Make sure you take part in the conversation, but encourage your partner to speak too.

Test 4

Paper 1 Reading and Writing (1 hour 30 minutes)

Reading
Part 1

Questions 1–5

Look at the text in each question.
What does it say?
Mark the correct letter **A, B** or **C** on your answer sheet.

Example:

0
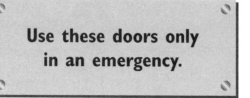

A You must never leave by these doors.

B The doors can be used if necessary.

C Only some people can use these doors.

Answer: | 0 | A   B   C |

1

> **This car park has 24-hour security cameras in operation.**

A The cameras are not operating at the moment.

B There is security in this car park day and night.

C This car park is only safe during the day.

2

> **If the ticket office is closed, please use the machines on the platform.**

A You can't always get a ticket from the machines.

B Tickets are available when the office isn't open.

C There are two ticket offices at this station.

Tip

You may see some of the same words in the sign and the options but the **whole** meaning must be the same in the correct option.

3

NOTICE

ALL MEMBERS

We are changing our Identity Cards. Could all members visit reception before April 15th to have their photos re-taken. Thank you.

The manager

A   All members have to have new identity cards.

B   Members should hand in new photos by April 15th.

C   Everybody must leave their identity cards at reception.

4

MESSAGE

To: Lisa
From: Janet

Lisa – Have you done your homework? I left my book at school! Can I use yours?

What does Janet want Lisa to do?

A   go to the school with her

B   explain the homework

C   lend her a book

5

Please show your staff discount card before you pay for your goods.

A   Some people can have a discount in this shop.

B   Staff are not allowed any discounts.

C   Staff will always ask you for your discount card.

Part 2

Questions 6–10

The people below are all planning a holiday.
On the opposite page there are descriptions of eight holidays.
Decide which holiday would be the most suitable for the following people.
For questions **6–10**, mark the correct letter (**A–H**) on your answer sheet.

Tip ————
Some of the information about the people and the choices A–H may be similar. Choose the **most suitable** answer each time.
————

6  Hannah is a computer programmer who works long hours. She is quite unfit at the moment, but would like to go on an activities holiday that allows her to try different sports.

7  Alberto needs a rest after his exams, but he doesn't want to go to the beach. He'd like to find a holiday that combines opportunities to relax with the chance to visit more than one country.

8  Charlotte is keen on sea life. She'd like to go on a holiday that allows her to explore underwater with other experienced divers.

9  Sue would prefer to go somewhere near the sea and stay in one place. She likes to do a variety of things when she's on holiday, including exploring the local area.

10  Simone and Pedro like to travel around on interesting forms of transport and they enjoy sightseeing and the countryside. This year they'd like to explore one country.

HOLIDAY CHOICE

A   Desert Island Dream

Visit the tiny island of Tobago for beautiful beaches. Watch the giant turtles, visit the rainforest, walk through the food markets, take a cruise. You'll never get bored in Tobago.

B   Breaks in France

With up to three days away, our short holidays give you plenty of time to try the restaurants of Normandy and do all your shopping!

C   Sun and Surf!

The wind in your hair, the sun on your face! Learn to windsurf, try diving, have a swim or soak up the sun on the deck of a yacht and watch the dolphins as you cruise from bay to bay.

D   Voyages of Discovery

Chase the sun around the Mediterranean on our seven-night cruise. Cross time zones overnight and wake up in different countries. Go sightseeing or stay on board. Life slows down at sea, you have time to think, read and best of all do absolutely nothing.

E   Explore the countryside

We offer fantastic canal holidays and canal boat hire on comfortable traditional boats. Float past woods, fields, pretty villages and historic towns and the finest English scenery. A great and original way to experience England.

F   Deep Down Under the Sea

Learn to deep-sea dive in the Caribbean. Price includes flight, hotel, teaching and equipment hire. No experience is necessary but please bring a medical certificate to show that you are fit and healthy!

G   Real Adventure

Have an adventure watching whales and dolphins. Beware! This trip is not for beginners or for those who simply want a ride on a boat! Along with our skilled crew you'll be expected to join in with plenty of hard work both on board and under the sea!

H   The sea – and nothing else

Choose from Greece, Turkey, or the Caribbean for a five day non-stop cruise on board one of our luxury liners. Enjoy the on-board entertainment and eat in top restaurants. You won't want to get off!

Part 3

Questions 11–20

Look at the sentences below about a gym that has recently opened.
Read the text on the opposite page to decide if each sentence is correct or incorrect.
If it is correct, mark **A** on your answer sheet.
If it is not correct, mark **B** on your answer sheet.

11 You are given an identity card as soon as you join the gymnasium.

12 Other people can use your membership card.

13 A programme is organised for each member on their first visit.

14 You must wear certain kinds of clothes in the gym.

15 You must take a towel into the gymnasium.

16 You can spend as long as you like on all equipment.

17 Staff are always able to answer your questions.

18 You can leave personal items at the gymnasium for 24 hours.

19 You must pay for food in the café.

20 All complaints should be made directly to the receptionist.

Fighting Fit Health Club

Membership Card

Fighting Fit is a members only club. When you first join, we give you a computerised card. This has your name and membership number
5 on. We also take your photo and use it for your identity card, which takes a few days to make.

Please have your card with you every time you use the club. The card is for your use only, and
10 there is a small charge to provide a new one if you lose it. Members are permitted to bring guests to use the facilities at the club. A visiting guest fee is charged for each guest.

Fitness Programmes

15 Your Fitness Programme includes a meeting with one of our skilled instructors. This will happen two or three weeks after you have joined. The instructor looks at your health, your current needs and the way you live, and
20 organises a programme suitable for you.

Gymnasium

Our gymnasiums are the most modern in the area and have high quality exercise equipment. For safety reasons, sportswear and
25 trainers must be worn while exercising, and please remember to take a small towel into the gymnasium too. It is one of our rules that you wipe the equipment after use.

There is no limit to how long you spend in the
30 gymnasium, but we ask you to respect other members by only spending 20 minutes on each piece of equipment. There are experienced staff in the gymnasiums at all times, who will help you with the equipment and your
35 exercise programme, and answer your questions. You can make a half-hour appointment to discuss your progress if you prefer.

Locker Rooms

We have large male and female locker rooms. 40 Please ensure that your property is kept in your locker at all times. Any belongings which are found either in a locker or anywhere else overnight will be removed and taken to Lost Property. We cannot be responsible for any 45 items which are lost in the club.

Café

The café offers a relaxing space where you can help yourselves to free tea, coffee and soft drinks. You will also find cold snacks including 50 sandwiches and a range of delicious salads at a very low cost.

Suggestion Box

Members' suggestions, and comments – good or bad – are always welcome, and the 55 suggestion box and forms can be found at reception. Please include your name and your membership number together with your comments. We try to respond within two days.

Tip

Don't worry if you don't understand some of the words – you may still be able to answer the questions.

Part 4

Questions 21–25

Read the text and questions below.
For each question, mark the correct letter **A, B, C** or **D** on your answer sheet.

Learn Indian Dancing

I've always wanted to learn how to dance. When I was younger, I loved going to discos and I used to spend hours practising my moves in front of the mirror! I think I was quite good, but as I got older, I became less confident.

Recently I decided I'd join a dance class. The problem with most dance classes is that you need
5 a partner, and none of my male friends ever wanted to come with me. I was beginning to give up on the idea when I came across a magazine article about Indian dancing. It sounded great and best of all I could do it on my own! So, I found a class on the internet and booked myself onto a course.

I turned up for our first lesson feeling very nervous. I needn't have worried though because
10 everyone was really friendly. We were all female, the youngest was about eighteen and the oldest was forty something.

Our teacher came in looking fantastic in her traditional dance clothes and we soon all caught her energy and enthusiasm. She put on the music immediately which was a combination of western pop songs set to an Indian beat, and we started following her moves. Any nervousness
15 soon disappeared because the moves are so complicated. There's no time to worry about whether you're doing them right!

I've noticed a lot of changes about myself since I started dancing. I'm much fitter and I feel more confident. I've also made some great friends at the class. If you're interested in dancing, or you just want to feel fitter, I'd recommend Indian dance!

21 What is the writer's main purpose in writing the text?

    A to describe her childhood

    B to say how she began her hobby

    C to explain why she likes dancing

    D to talk about the people she has met

22 What would a reader learn about the writer from the text?

    A She is good at Indian dancing.

    B She enjoys dancing.

    C She likes listening to pop music.

    D She's interested in keeping fit.

23 What does the writer say about herself?

    A She hasn't always been confident.

    B She doesn't enjoy doing new things.

    C She likes meeting people.

    D She was a very nervous child.

24 What does the writer say about the first dance class?

    A Everybody was keen to dance.

    B Nobody spoke to each other at first.

    C Everybody admired the teacher.

    D A lot of time was spent discussing the moves.

25 Which advert do you think the writer found on the internet?

A

> **Learn how to dance! No experience necessary! No need to bring a partner! We'll match you with somebody when you arrive!**

B

> **Have you always wanted to learn how to dance? We teach you simple steps from Latin American to Indian dancing.**

C

> **If you're interested in dance why not learn the art of Indian dancing! Friendly classes! Excellent teachers! Everybody welcome!**

D

> **Are you bored with doing the same old thing? Persuade your partner to join a dance class! Have fun and keep fit at the same time!**

Tip

Remember that the choices may have similar meanings or contain similar information to the text. The right answer must be **completely** correct.

Part 5

Questions 26–35

Read the text below and choose the correct word for each space.
For each question, mark the correct letter **A**, **B**, **C** or **D** on your answer sheet.

Example:

0 A chance   **B** manner   **C** method   **D** way

Answer: 0 | A B C **D**

Body Language

Many people believe the **(0)** .... to really know somebody is to understand what they mean when they're saying **(26)** .... at all! This is the science of **(27)** .... body language. In **(28)** ...., learning how to recognise body language and how to use it to communicate your **(29)** .... message, is big business. **(30)** .... there are hundreds of books written on the subject.

Experts are even going into companies to talk **(31)** .... employees about how to perform better. They suggest that this can be done with a **(32)** .... changes in their body-talk. Welcoming body language, for example, **(33)** .... to include giving a friendly nod to say hello and leaning forward slightly to show you want to listen. The problem is, the more we understand body language, the more able we are to change it if we want to. This means that realising when somebody is **(34)** .... a lie is more difficult than **(35)** .... used to be!

26 **A** anything   **B** nothing   **C** something   **D** no one

27 **A** getting   **B** realising   **C** understanding   **D** seeing

28 **A** order   **B** case   **C** spite   **D** fact

29 **A** every   **B** only   **C** single   **D** own

30 **A** Nowadays   **B** Daily   **C** Often   **D** Previously

31 **A** at   **B** for   **C** to   **D** by

32 **A** few   **B** several   **C** many   **D** some

33 **A** should   **B** can   **C** might   **D** ought

34 **A** telling   **B** saying   **C** speaking   **D** talking

35 **A** its   **B** it   **C** they   **D** them

Tip

Look at the words before and after the gap for help.

Writing
Part 1

Questions 1–5

Here are some sentences about television.
For each question, complete the second sentence so that it means the same as the first.
Use no more than three words.
Write only the missing words on your answer sheet.
You may use this page for any rough work.

Example:

0 We left the cinema because the film was so boring.

It was .... **a boring film that we left the cinema.**

Answer: | 0 | *such* |

---

1 You should switch off the TV and do something more interesting.

If I were you .... **switch off the TV and do something more interesting.**

2 When I was a child I loved watching cartoons.

I used .... **watching cartoons when I was a child.**

> *Tip*
>
> Be careful with verbs. Make sure that the tense or form you write is correct.

3 I prefer watching films to watching documentaries.

I like watching films .... **watching documentaries.**

4 That programme was made in America.

They .... **that programme in America.**

5 I find games shows boring.

I get .... **by game shows.**

Part 2

Question 6

You are going to visit your aunt in the countryside.
Write a card to your aunt. In your card, you should
- thank her for the invitation
- say when you're going to arrive
- describe what you hope to do there.

Write **35–45 words** on your answer sheet.

Tip

Remember to include all three parts of the question. Don't put in too many of your own ideas.

Part 3

Write an answer to **one** of the questions (**7** or **8**) in this part.
Write your answer in about **100 words** on your answer sheet.
Put the question number in the box at the top of your answer sheet.

Question 7

- This is part of a letter you receive from your English friend.

> In your next letter, please tell me all
> about your home. Where is it? What
> do you like about it?

- Now write a letter answering your friend's questions.
- Write your **letter** on your answer sheet.

Tip

Write suitable sentences to open and close your letter e.g. 'Thank you for your letter', 'How are you?' and 'See you soon', 'Write to me soon'.

Question 8

- Your English teacher has asked you to write a story.
- Your story must begin with this sentence:

I opened the door very slowly.

- Write your **story** on your answer sheet.

Tip

Remember to use past tenses when telling a story.

Paper 2   Listening (about 30 minutes)
Part 1

Questions 1–7

There are seven questions in this part.
For each question there are three pictures and a short recording.
Choose the correct picture and put a tick (✔) in the box below it.

Example: How does the woman travel to work?

A ☐   B ✔   C ☐

1 What is the woman going to read on the plane?

A ☐   B ☐   C ☐

2 What will Mr Brown find at the desk?

A ☐   B ☐   C ☐

3 Where is the hotel?

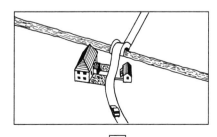

A ☐   B ☐   C ☐

4 How did the woman hear from James?

A ☐

B ☐

C ☐

5 What is the date of the marathon?

A ☐

B ☐

C ☐

6 What's the weather going to be like tomorrow?

A ☐

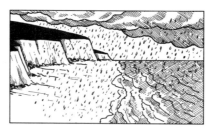

B ☐

C ☐

7 What are they going to eat tonight?

A ☐

B ☐

C ☐

Part 2

Questions 8–13

You will hear someone talking about summer activities.
For each question, put a tick (✔) in the correct box.

Tip

Don't choose an answer just because you hear a word from it on the recording.

8 What does the presenter say about the Triple Theatre Company?

A They do a variety of activities. ☐

B They may cancel their appearance. ☐

C Their performance last year was disappointing. ☐

9 Open air concerts are held

A every week in July. ☐

B more than once in July. ☐

C only in July. ☐

10 One performance of *Twelfth Night* is cancelled because

A the weather is likely to be bad. ☐

B not enough people bought tickets. ☐

C the actors have to be somewhere else. ☐

11 The concert at the weekend water festival will take place

A on a boat. ☐

B on a bridge. ☐

C in a tent. ☐

12 What is true about people taking part in the talent show?

A They must be under eighteen. ☐

B Their performance must last for less than ten minutes. ☐

C They must have applied to take part. ☐

13 What is different about this year's film festival?

A Food will be served all night. ☐

B It will take place in the park. ☐

C There will be an entry fee. ☐

Part 3

Questions 14–19

You will hear somebody welcoming a group of international students to a college.
For each question, fill in the missing information in the numbered space.

Highdown College
Accommodation

Office at the college **(14)** ....

Opening hours – term time:

Monday – Friday

9 a.m. to 4 p.m.

(Holidays: Monday and **(15)** .... mornings only)

Emergency No. **(16)** ....

College facilities

Learning Resource Centre – over 50,000 library books

50 **(17)** .... with internet facilities

Snacks (including sandwiches and **(18)** ....) – in The Hungry Café on the first floor

Hot meals – in The Food Hall on the ground floor next to the **(19)** ....

Pub lunch – in the Students' Bar

Tip ———————

You will hear the exact word you
need for the answer, but the words
or sentence you hear **around** it may
not be exactly the same as on the
question paper.

———————

Part 4

Questions 20–25

Look at the six sentences for this part.
You will hear a conversation between a girl, Jodie, and a boy, Harry, about exams.
Decide if each sentence is correct or incorrect.
If it is correct, put a tick (✔) in the box under **A** for **YES**. If it is not correct, put a tick (✔) in the box under **B** for **NO**.

Tip

If you miss the answer to one question, leave it and think about the next one, but make sure you tick the box for the right question number. You can check your answers and any you missed on the second listening.

	A YES	B NO
20 Harry has been going out a lot recently.	☐	☐
21 Harry always works hard.	☐	☐
22 Jodie is confident about her exams.	☐	☐
23 Jodie thinks studying all night is sometimes useful.	☐	☐
24 Harry agrees he needs to do more exercise.	☐	☐
25 Harry promises to go to the party.	☐	☐

Paper 3 Speaking (10–12 minutes)

Part 1 Personal information (2–3 minutes)

Answer these questions:
What's your name?
What's your surname? How do you spell it?
Where do you live?
Do you work or are you a student?
Do you enjoy studying English?
Do you think that English will be useful to you in the future?
What do you enjoy doing in your free time?

Tip

You may have to give numbers, e.g. your telephone number. Make sure you can say them properly, and be careful with numbers you know are difficult.

Part 2 Simulated situation (2–3 minutes)

You are spending the evening with a friend who you have not seen for a long time.
Look at the picture on page 75.
Talk about what you could do and decide what would be the most suitable.

Tip

Try to say something about as many of the pictures as you can but don't worry if you don't have enough time.

Part 3 Responding to a photograph (3 minutes)

Candidate A: look at Photo 1 on page 95, show it to Candidate B and talk about it.
Candidate B: look at Photo 2 on page 96, show it to Candidate A and talk about it.

Tip

If you aren't sure about things in the photo, use expressions like 'I think', 'It looks like', 'It might/could be', etc.

Part 4 General conversation based on the photographs (3 minutes)

Talk to each other about your favourite season.
Talk about what you enjoy doing at different times of year.

Tip

It doesn't matter if you agree or disagree with what your partner says. It is a discussion, not an argument!

Test 5

Paper 1 Reading and Writing (1 hour 30 minutes)

Reading
Part 1

Questions 1–5

Look at the text in each question.
What does it say?
Mark the correct letter **A**, **B** or **C** on your answer sheet.

Example:

0

> ## Use these doors only in an emergency.

A You must never leave by these doors.

B The doors can be used if necessary.

C Only some people can use these doors.

Answer: | 0 | A   B   C |

1

> Jaques
> Can you tell Louisa I can't go out tonight? I've lost her phone number and I don't know her address! Thanks.
> Marco

What does Marco want Jaques to do?

A tell him Louisa's phone number

B give somebody a message

C visit Louisa at home

2

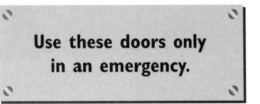

> *Please ask at hotel reception for a copy of our winter prices.*

A The price of some rooms has increased.

B Prices are the same all year.

C The receptionist has a list of how much rooms cost.

3

Warning

Road works starting next month.
Please use other routes where
possible.

A   There are traffic problems on this route today.

B   You should start planning to travel a different way.

C   There will be delays for the next four weeks.

4

NOTICE

Exam Students

Please hand in your entry forms by 16th
March. Anyone who does not will not be
entered for the exam.

A   You can only take the exam if you have completed an entry form.

B   It is possible to take the exam if you give in a form after 16th March.

C   You cannot take the exam if you have failed it before.

Tip

If there are negative words like *no, not, no one,* etc. think carefully about the meaning.

5

MESSAGE

To: Jaime
From: Your English Teacher

Jaime – The bus didn't arrive and
there isn't another one for thirty
minutes. We'll add an extra hour to
next week's lesson instead.

Jaime's English teacher is going to

A   cancel next week's lesson.

B   increase the time of next week's lesson.

C   arrive late for next week's lesson.

Part 2

Questions 6–10

The people below are all planning to take up a new activity.
On the opposite page there are descriptions of eight classes.
Decide which class would be the most suitable for the following people.
For questions **6–10**, mark the correct letter (**A–H**) on your answer sheet.

Tip
When you have chosen your answers, check once again that the three you haven't used from A–H don't match any of the people.

6 Pablo works with computers and feels he needs to do something that will keep him fit. He isn't sure what to do so he'd like to be able to try an activity before making a final decision.

7  Sally is a waitress and works a lot of hours at different times of the day and evening. She'd like to be able to do something creative in her own time.

8  Maria is a student and would like do an activity during the day. She enjoys team games and is keen to play regularly.

9  Robert wants to take up an activity that will give him plenty of contact with other people. He is confident and enjoys performing.

10  Helen has a busy and stressful job and wants to find a way of relaxing that she can also do at home. She wants to look better and feel better!

Free Time

A Art Scene

You don't have to be Picasso to learn to draw and paint in a friendly and relaxed atmosphere. Our evening course includes trips to art galleries and visits by local artists.

B Pen to Paper

To help you become a first-class writer, we offer you a home-study course. We have excellent tutors who will guide you through the course and show you how to make the most of your ability. Write and study when and where you want. It couldn't be easier.

C Mind and Body

Try yoga to help you deal with life's worries! It can also help improve the way you look and develop concentration. Best of all, once you've learned the basics, it's something you can do anywhere.

D Lunchtime Fun

Fed up with sitting about in your lunch hour wondering what to do? Get your sports clothes on and come down to Rivertime Leisure Centre for lunchtime basketball. Every Tuesday and Thursday.

E Get started in IT

If you're interested in computers and you're not sure what direction to take, try a weekend course at one of our centres. Get familiar with computer basics, then move on to one of our 12-week courses.

F What's Cooking?

Would you like to create fantastic meals and dinner parties for your friends, or do you simply have trouble making an omelette? If the answer is 'yes' to either of these questions, why not try one of our Friday evening cooking classes? You'll always have ideas for the weekend!

G Salsa for Beginners

Dancing is great exercise! Find out if it's for you with our free 'Salsa for Beginners'. Spend an hour having fun in a lively class. We're sure you'll want to book straight onto one of our courses after that!

H On Stage

If you'd like something new and interesting to do, why not join the Talking Theatre Group? We work hard but we have a lot of fun too! We put on two shows a year for local people, which are always very popular.

Part 3

Questions 11–20

Look at the sentences below about trips to the Great Bear Rainforest.
Read the text on the opposite page to decide if each sentence is correct or incorrect.
If it is correct, mark **A** on your answer sheet.
If it is not correct, mark **B** on your answer sheet.

___

11 The Great Bear Rainforest is divided into several parts.

12 Spirit Bears can only be found in the Great Bear Rainforest.

13 You can have various kinds of holiday on the island.

14 People who live in the area welcome tourists.

15 The bears appear when the fish are returning to the Pacific Ocean.

16 Knight Inlet is in the middle of the rainforest.

17 Guests at Knight Inlet travel straight to the river by boat.

18 There is a choice of places to see the bears from.

19 Tourists can watch the bears all year round.

20 All tourists must sleep more than one night at Campbell River.

Tip _____

Check your answers carefully: match the words you underlined in 11–20 with the meaning in the text.

Explore The Great Bear Rainforest

The Great Bear Rainforest is on an island on British Columbia's central coast, in Canada. The rainforest is the largest remaining piece of unbroken rainforest in the world and is full of interesting plants, birds and

5 animals, including the Spirit Bear. It is thought that there are no more than 400 of these bears in the whole of the Great Bear Rainforest – and they don't exist anywhere else in the world.

The Island is a fantastic place to go bear and whale

10 watching. It is also a great place to go diving, snorkelling and fishing. Even better, tourism is encouraged by local people and conservationists, as it shows that money can be made from the island without changing it, and this helps to protect the rainforest.

One of the best times to visit the island is mid-September. This is when salmon return in great numbers from

15 the Pacific Ocean to the streams and rivers of British Columbia's west coast. It is also when the bears come out to hunt them!

Knight Inlet is a place well known for its population of grizzly bears. It is on the southern edge of the Great Bear Rainforest. There can be up to 40 bears within a few miles during autumn when the fish are swimming up the river. Guests who stay at Knight Inlet start their adventure with a boat ride. They then board a small

20 bus and travel through the northern rainforest to the river. They can go to five different viewing platforms, in three different areas, which are specially built to provide a safe and comfortable place to watch the bears from. It is not uncommon to see 10–15 bears on the river at a time.

Autumn isn't the only season that grizzly bears go to the area. Starting in April, when they've woken from their winter sleep, both black and grizzly bears arrive to feed on the new spring growth. Even in mid-summer,

25 when many of the bears have moved into the forests for their food, you can see several bears each day.

Knight Inlet offers wildlife viewing holidays ranging from one to seven nights for our spring,

30 summer and autumn bear viewing. All their holidays begin at Campbell River and include one night in one of the two hotels there. This is essential because the plane journey to Knight Inlet starts very early in the morning.

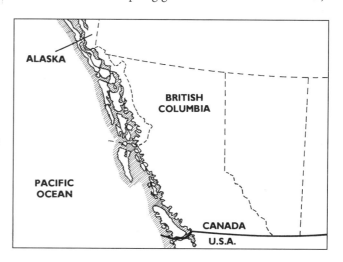

Part 4

Questions 21–25

Read the text and questions below.
For each question, mark the correct letter **A**, **B**, **C** or **D** on your answer sheet.

Are you shopping too much?

Shopping used to be my favourite activity. It started when I was a teenager and I
worked in a clothes shop. I had a staff discount in the shop and I used to spend all my
wages on clothes. When I got a job in an office I carried on spending all my spare
money on clothes – even after I had got married, bought a house and had children!

5   I used to go shopping every weekend and I probably spent about £500 a month on
clothes. It wasn't something I only did when I wasn't very happy, I always went
shopping however I felt. Sometimes I'd look for ages to find what I wanted. Other
times, I'd just buy the first thing I saw.

Most of the things I didn't need. One day I bought three pairs of boots, even though I
10   already had another ten pairs at home. I never even took the most expensive pair out of
the box!

I realised I had a problem when one day my five-year-old daughter looked into my
wardrobe and asked me why I had so many handbags. I counted them. I had seventy-
five handbags and they must have cost me thousands of pounds. I couldn't believe what
15   I'd done!

First of all, I threw away my credit card. Then I gave away all the clothes that I'd never
worn. After that I made arrangements every Saturday to visit friends or go on a day
trip, so I wouldn't be able to go shopping.

21 What is the writer's main aim in writing the text?

    A to advise people how to shop sensibly

    B to talk about her expensive way of living

    C to describe her addiction to shopping

    D to talk about different fashions

22 What does the writer say about herself after
she got married?

    A She tried to stop spending so much.

    B She managed to spend less than before.

    C She continued spending unwisely.

    D She became depressed about her spending.

23 What does the writer say about her past shopping habits?

A She only bought expensive clothes.

B She always thought carefully about what she bought.

C She liked to buy something different every day.

D She sometimes bought things she already had.

24 How did the writer feel when she realised she had a problem?

A shocked

B embarrassed

C angry with herself

D miserable

25 Which of the following is the best description of the writer?

A The woman who grew up loving clothes and looked fantastic in everything she wore.

B The woman who recognised her problem but failed to change herself.

C The woman who loved collecting clothes and succeeded in fighting her habit.

D The woman who shopped and shopped until she had no money left to spend.

Tip

Before you decide on your answer, check once again that the other choices are not correct.

Part 5

Questions 26–35

Read the text below and choose the correct word for each space.
For each question, mark the correct letter **A, B, C** or **D** on your answer sheet.

Example:

0 A in   **B** on   **C** at   **D** of

Answer:

0	A	B	C	D
	▬	▭	▭	▭

The Cannes Film Festival

The Cannes Film Festival is the most famous film festival **(0)** .... the world. **(26)** .... a film is presented there it is immediately famous. The festival is **(27)** .... where some of the film industry's most important business takes place and where many actors and directors **(28)** .... stars.

The **(29)** .... began in 1939 when the French government **(30)** .... to have an international festival. They chose Cannes, **(31)** .... is in southern France, because it is a sunny and beautiful town. In fact, Cannes was **(32)** .... seen as a fashionable place to go. The festival was put **(33)** .... until after the war and finally took place on September 20, 1946. At **(34)** ...., the festival was mainly a tourist and a social event. However, as more and more films were **(35)** .... it was seen as something much more important. Today it has become the most important event of the year for the film industry.

---

26 A Although   **B** Whether   **C** If   **D** As

27 A and   **B** too   **C** also   **D** else

28 A become   **B** turn   **C** get   **D** change

29 A fact   **B** idea   **C** opinion   **D** view

30 A decided   **B** thought   **C** considered   **D** wondered

31 A where   **B** what   **C** who   **D** which

32 A yet   **B** even   **C** already   **D** ever

33 A off   **B** away   **C** on   **D** through

34 A least   **B** first   **C** once   **D** last

35 A done   **B** had   **C** tried   **D** shown

Tip

When you have finished read the whole text again to check your answers make sense.

Writing
Part 1

Questions 1–5

Here are some sentences about free time.
For each question, complete the second sentence so that it means the same as the first.
Use no more than three words.
Write only the missing words on your answer sheet.
You may use this page for any rough work.

Example:

0 It was a really boring film.

    It wasn't a very .... **film.**

Answer: | 0 | *interesting* |

---

1 That café has better food than any other café in the area.

    That café has .... **food in the area.**

> *Tip* ━━━━━━━━━━
>
> Check your answer has **exactly** the same meaning as the first sentence. Don't leave anything out.
>
> ━━━━━━━━━━

2 It's too cold to go for a walk.

    It isn't warm .... **to go for a walk.**

3 There are three screens at that cinema.

    That cinema .... **three screens.**

4 You must turn off your phones during the performance.

    You are not *Allowed* **to have your phones turned on during the performance.**

5 Only students can get discounts.

    You can only get a discount .... **a student.**

Part 2

Question 6

You are on holiday in another country.
Write a card to your English friend, Jim. In your card, you should
- tell him where you are staying
- say what you are doing
- suggest you meet when you return.

Write **35–45 words** on your answer sheet.

Tip _____

Read your answer carefully. Check the number of words and your spelling and grammar.

Part 3

Write an answer to **one** of the questions (**7** or **8**) in this part.
Write your answer in about **100 words** on your answer sheet.
Put the question number in the box at the top of your answer sheet.

Question 7

- Your English teacher has asked you to write a story.
- Your story must begin with this sentence:

   Late in the evening I heard a loud knock on the door.

- Write your **story** on your answer sheet.

Tip _____

Check your answer carefully for spelling and grammar.

Question 8

- This is part of a letter you receive from your English friend, Mark.

  In your next letter, please tell me about your family. Do you spend much time together? Do you have any brothers and sisters?

- Now write a letter to Mark, answering his questions.
- Write your **letter** on your answer sheet.

Tip _____

There are usually two or three parts to the question. Answer all of them and don't write **too many** of your own ideas.

Paper 2   Listening (about 30 minutes)
Part 1

Tip

Mark in pencil the answer you think is right. Check it on the second listening. Don't worry if you can't do one question, leave it and go on to the next one.

Questions 1–7

There are seven questions in this part.
For each question there are three pictures and a short recording.
Choose the correct picture and put a tick (✔) in the box below it.

Example: How does the woman travel to work?

A ☐   B ✔   C ☐

---

1 What will the weather be like tomorrow?

A ☐   B ☐   C ☐

2 How did Sarah get home last night?

A ☐   B ☐   C ☐

3 What would the man like to do on his birthday?

A ☐   B ☐   C ☐

4 Which book did the woman buy?

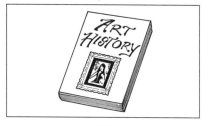

A

B

C

5 What time does the supermarket close today?

A

B

C

6 Where is Mary?

A

B

C

7 Where are they going to meet?

A

B

C

Part 2

Questions 8–13

You will hear an interview with an organiser at a tennis club.
For each question, put a tick (✔) in the correct box.

8 Chris hopes to

   A encourage people to join the club. ☐

   B discover new talented players. ☐

   C find more people to teach players. ☐

9 What does Chris say about club nights?

   A They are held only in the summer. ☐

   B There is sometimes a small charge. ☐

   C Refreshments are provided each night. ☐

10 The teaching programme

   A is offered to people with membership only. ☐

   B is available to people wanting to learn on their own. ☐

   C must be paid for in advance. ☐

11 From spring, the tennis club is going to

   A introduce junior club night. ☐

   B encourage parents to help with teaching. ☐

   C provide snacks on junior club night. ☐

12 Who is responsible for organising the club nights?

   A unpaid members ☐

   B various office workers ☐

   C the teaching staff ☐

13 The junior competition is

   A intended as practice for more serious competitions. ☐

   B for advanced players only. ☐

   C held in March. ☐

Tip

When you tick the box make it clear so you are sure of your answers when you write them on the answer sheet. Make sure you put the right answer with the right question number.

Part 3

Questions 14–19

You will hear somebody talking about trips on the river. For each question, fill in the missing information in the numbered space.

Tip

If the answer is a number, you can write a word or a number. Be careful with numbers like 13 and 30.

River Cruises

Private parties

Groups: Minimum 10 people

              Maximum **(14)** .... people

Available all year round

Trips last 2–5 hours in the evening or **(15)** ....

Food: Cold buffet or **(16)** ....

              Must be ordered at least **(17)** .... before

Cost

Boat hire includes disco or **(18)** ....

Extra cost for live entertainment

Bookings:

Through website, by telephone or at the **(19)** .... in the leisure centre.

Part 4

Questions 20–25

Look at the six sentences for this part.
You will hear a conversation between a girl, Maria, and a boy, Dominic, about keeping fit.
Decide if each sentence is correct or incorrect.
If it is correct, put a tick (✔) in the box under **A** for **YES**. If it is not correct, put a tick (✔) in the box under **B** for **NO**.

Tip
Make sure you know who is speaking.
There will always be one male and one
female speaker.

		A	B
		YES	NO
20	Maria and Dominic agree that running a marathon would be enjoyable.	☐	☐
21	Maria is worried that running will be boring.	☐	☐
22	Maria regularly does exercise classes.	☐	☐
23	Dominic thinks Maria will feel uncomfortable running in public.	☐	☐
24	Dominic would feel happier running alone.	☐	☐
25	Dominic thinks Maria needs to make an effort.	☐	☐

Paper 3 Speaking (10–12 minutes)

Part 1 Personal information (2–3 minutes)

Answer these questions:
What's your name?
What's your surname? How do you spell it?
Where do you live?
Do you work or are you a student?
Do you enjoy studying English?
Do you think that English will be useful to you in the future?
What do you enjoy doing in your free time?

Tip

Wait for the examiner to ask you a question. Try to answer with a whole sentence, not one word.

Part 2 Simulated situation (2–3 minutes)

Your teacher has asked you for ideas to improve your school.
Look at the picture on page 93.
Talk about what improvements you think would be most useful.

Tip

Try to reach an agreement with your partner, but don't worry if you can't agree. The important thing is that you talk to each other.

Part 3 Responding to a visual stimulus (3 minutes)

Candidate A: look at Photo 1 on page 97, show it to Candidate B and talk about it.
Candidate B: look at Photo 2 on page 98, show it to Candidate A and talk about it.

Tip

Don't just list the things you can see. Talk about **who** the person is, **where** they are, **what** they are doing, **why** they are doing it, etc.

Part 4 General conversation based on the photographs (3 minutes)

Talk to each other about where and when you go shopping.
Talk about what you like about shopping and what you don't like.

Tip

Try to relax and enjoy the conversation. Don't worry if you make some mistakes. The important thing is to keep talking.

Test 1 Part 3 Photo 1

Test 3 Part 3 Photo 2

Test 1   Part 3   Photo 2

Test 4   Part 3   Photo 1

Test 2 Part 3 Photo 1

Test 4 Part 3 Photo 2

Test 2 Part 3 Photo 2

Test 5 Part 3 Photo 1

Test 3 Part 3 Photo 1

Test 5 Part 3 Photo 2

UNIVERSITY *of* CAMBRIDGE
ESOL Examinations

Candidate Name
If not already printed, write name
in CAPITALS and complete the
Candidate No. grid (in pencil).

Candidate Signature

Examination Title

Centre

Supervisor:
If the candidate is ABSENT or has WITHDRAWN shade here ⊐

SAMPLE

Centre No.

Candidate No.

Examination Details

0	0	0	0
1	1	1	1
2	2	2	2
3	3	3	3
4	4	4	4
5	5	5	5
6	6	6	6
7	7	7	7
8	8	8	8
9	9	9	9

PET Paper 1 Reading and Writing Candidate Answer Sheet 1

Instructions

Use a PENCIL (B or HB).

Rub out any answer you want to change with an eraser.

For **Reading:**
Mark ONE letter for each question.
For example, if you think **A** is the right answer to the
question, mark your answer sheet like this:

0 | A B C D

Part 1	Part 2	Part 3	Part 4	Part 5
1 A B C	6 A B C D E F G H	11 A B	21 A B C D	26 A B C D
2 A B C	7 A B C D E F G H	12 A B	22 A B C D	27 A B C D
3 A B C	8 A B C D E F G H	13 A B	23 A B C D	28 A B C D
4 A B C	9 A B C D E F G H	14 A B	24 A B C D	29 A B C D
5 A B C	10 A B C D E F G H	15 A B	25 A B C D	30 A B C D
		16 A B		31 A B C D
		17 A B		32 A B C D
		18 A B		33 A B C D
		19 A B		34 A B C D
		20 A B		35 A B C D

Continue on the other side of this sheet ➡

PET RW 1   DP491/389

For **Writing (Parts 1 and 2):**

Write your answers clearly in the spaces provided.

SAMPLE

Part 1: Write your answers below.	Do not write here
1	1 1 0
2	1 2 0
3	1 3 0
4	1 4 0
5	1 5 0

Part 2 (Question 6): Write your answer below.

Put your answer to Writing Part 3 on Answer Sheet 2 →

Do not write below (Examiner use only)					
0	1	2	3	4	5

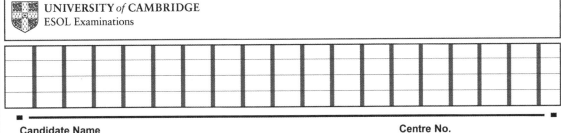

UNIVERSITY *of* CAMBRIDGE
ESOL Examinations

Candidate Name
If not already printed, write name
in CAPITALS and complete the
Candidate No. grid (in pencil).

Candidate Signature

Examination Title

Centre

Supervisor:
If the candidate is ABSENT or has WITHDRAWN shade here ⊂⊐

SAMPLE

Centre No.

Candidate No.

Examination
Details

0	0	0	0
1	1	1	1
2	2	2	2
3	3	3	3
4	4	4	4
5	5	5	5
6	6	6	6
7	7	7	7
8	8	8	8
9	9	9	9

PET Paper 1 Reading and Writing   Candidate Answer Sheet 2

Candidate Instructions:

**Write your answer to Writing Part 3
on the other side of this sheet.**

➡

Use a PENCIL (B or HB).

This section for use by FIRST Examiner only

Mark:

| 0 | 1.1 | 1.2 | 1.3 | 2.1 | 2.2 | 2.3 | 3.1 | 3.2 | 3.3 | 4.1 | 4.2 | 4.3 | 5.1 | 5.2 | 5.3 |
| ⊐ | ⊐ | ⊐ | ⊐ | ⊐ | ⊐ | ⊐ | ⊐ | ⊐ | ⊐ | ⊐ | ⊐ | ⊐ | ⊐ | ⊐ | ⊐ |

Examiner Number:

	0 1 2 3 4 5 6 7 8 9
	0 1 2 3 4 5 6 7 8 9
	0 1 2 3 4 5 6 7 8 9
	0 1 2 3 4 5 6 7 8 9

PET RW 2

DP492/390

© UCLES 2003

Part 3: Mark the number of the question you are answering here ➡ $\underset{\rule{0.6em}{0.4pt}}{Q7}$ or $\underset{\rule{0.6em}{0.4pt}}{Q8}$

Write your answer below.

Do not write below this line

This section for use by SECOND Examiner only

Mark:

0	1.1	1.2	1.3	2.1	2.2	2.3	3.1	3.2	3.3	4.1	4.2	4.3	5.1	5.2	5.3

Examiner Number:

| 0 1 2 3 4 5 6 7 8 9 |
| 0 1 2 3 4 5 6 7 8 9 |
| 0 1 2 3 4 5 6 7 8 9 |
| 0 1 2 3 4 5 6 7 8 9 |

SAMPLE

Photocopiable

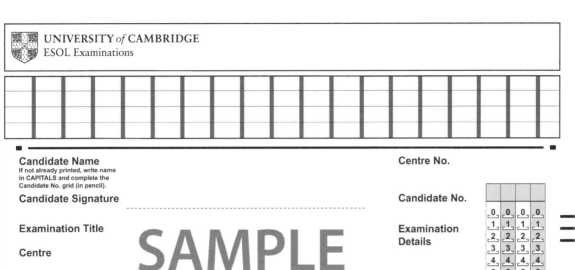

UNIVERSITY *of* **CAMBRIDGE**
ESOL Examinations

Candidate Name
If not already printed, write name
in CAPITALS and complete the
Candidate No. grid (in pencil).

Candidate Signature

Examination Title

Centre

Supervisor:
If the candidate is ABSENT or has WITHDRAWN shade here ▭

SAMPLE

Centre No.

Candidate No.

Examination Details

PET Paper 2 Listening Candidate Answer Sheet

You must transfer all your answers from the Listening Question Paper to this answer sheet.

Instructions

Use a PENCIL (B or HB).

Rub out any answer you want to change with an eraser.

For **Parts 1, 2** and **4:**
Mark ONE letter for each question.
For example, if you think **A** is the right answer to the
question, mark your answer sheet like this:

For **Part 3:**
Write your answers clearly in the spaces next
to the numbers (14 to 19) like this:

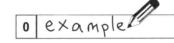

Part 1		Part 2		Part 3		Do not write here	Part 4	
1	A B C	8	A B C	14		1 14 0	20	A B
2	A B C	9	A B C	15		1 15 0	21	A B
3	A B C	10	A B C	16		1 16 0	22	A B
4	A B C	11	A B C	17		1 17 0	23	A B
5	A B C	12	A B C	18		1 18 0	24	A B
6	A B C	13	A B C	19		1 19 0	25	A B
7	A B C							

PET L

DP493/391

Key

Test 1

Paper 1 Reading and Writing

Reading

Part 1

1 B   2 A   3 C   4 C   5 B

Part 2

(The key words from each person are given opposite the key words from the answers.)

6 C

Anna	Riverstone Restaurant
Saturday night/chat/ hear some music	live music every Friday and Saturday night after 9 p.m.
have a good meal	wide selection of modern European dishes

7 D

Henri	Hollywood Stars
listen to music	live band and disco
lively place	have fun
meet new people	make new friends

8 B

George	70's Night
Friday night	Eight until late this Friday
music and dancing	70's disco music

9 E

Maria	Jazz and Stuff
all kinds of music	jazz, blues, country, soul, rock 'n' roll and pop
sit quietly and listen to some music	one of the best concerts

10 G

Carol	Upton Hotel and Restaurant
quiet place	quiet and pleasant hotel
where they can eat	exciting and creative menus
discuss ... the future of their company	business meetings

Part 3

11   **A Correct.** The tour begins *with the capital of the country, Lima* (l.1).

12   **A Correct.** There are organised tours that involve *sightseeing with our excellent guides* (l.6).

13   **B Incorrect.** You do not have to book before you arrive – you can *book any activity as soon as you arrive* (l.8).

14   **B Incorrect.** It is not non-stop because you *visit local villages and eat in local restaurants* (l.10).

15   **B Incorrect.** You do not pay more because *the full cost ... is included in the price of the tour* (l.12).

16   **B Incorrect.** There is not a choice in the mountains when you stay *together in local hotels* (l.14).

17   **B Incorrect.** There is no chance of a trip as there is *just enough time to eat and sleep* (l.16).

18   **A Correct.** There are opportunities to buy *local cloths and pots* (l.21).

19   **A Correct.** The trip includes a talk by *a traditional Peruvian band* (l.22).

20   **A Correct.** On the final day you can *visit the famous Gold Museum* (l.29).

Part 4

(The first answer given is always the correct one.)

21   **D** She talks about how to make exercise enjoyable to encourage people.
A x   She suggests some ways of keeping fit but this isn't the main aim.
B x   She says *Exercise is good for you* (l.2) so there is no need to persuade people of the benefits.
C x   She only talks about them briefly.

22   **C** She talks about the gym, jogging and modern dance.
A x   All the activities she talks about are done outside the home.
B x   She was bored of the same aerobics class (l.10) but has joined a dance class, which is *great fun* (l.14).
D x   When she says *a terrible TV programme* (l.6) she is talking about other people avoiding exercise.

23   **A** This is her recommendation (l.7).
B x   She says she's met lots of new people at the dance class (l.14) but doesn't say she exercises with friends.
C x   She never does aerobics (l.12).
D x   She often changes her route (l.11).

24   **B** She'll leave if she gets bored (l.15).
A x   She says it's great fun (l.14); as soon as she gets bored she'll leave but she isn't bored yet.
C x   This isn't mentioned.
D x   She suggests playing a sport (l.13) but doesn't say sport is better than dance.

25   **C** She recommends exercising three times a week.
A x   She thinks exercise doesn't need to be boring.
B x   She doesn't say this.
D x   She doesn't say this.

Part 5

26 B
A, C and D all need the article 'a'.
27 B
A, C and D are incorrect prepositions after *learn* in this context.
28 A
'Give someone the opportunity' means 'give someone the chance'. The other meanings are wrong here.
29 A
'Somewhere else' means 'in another place'. B, C and D do not follow *somewhere*.
30 D
While means 'during the time' or 'when'. A, B and C do not refer to a period of time.
31 C
A, B and D do not replace the noun *students*.
32 B
A, C and D do not make a phrase with *school*.
33 B
A, C and D describe plural nouns.
34 D
somebody means 'one particular person'. A and C are used in negatives and questions and B doesn't fit the meaning.
35 A
B, C and D all need 'to'.

Writing

Part 1

1 I wanted to improve my French **so** I went to France.
2 I get **embarrassed** when speaking in a foreign language.
3 I like speaking English **more/better than** writing it.
4 The teacher **who** taught me Italian was very good.
5 Languages are my **best** subject.

Part 2

Question 6: sample answer

> Dear Tom,
> How are you?
> Belive good!
> Thank you for your visit in my city because it was fanny and beautiful.
> I was very happy when I stay with you because you're very nice and intelligent person.
> Why this summer you don't come year?
> I miss you!!
> Bye Bye
>   Valentina

COMMENTS

3 marks

Valentina's first long sentence (*Thank you for your visit in my city ...*) does not communicate the first point well (thanking Tom for her stay at his place). The second part is clearly communicated – it is acceptable to say that what she enjoyed most was Tom's company. The wrong spelling of *here* in the last sentence makes the third point difficult to understand.

Part 3

Question 7: sample answer

> When I opened the letter, I found a plane ticket with my name on it. It was my sister's present: a plain ticket to go to her home in London. I immediately show the present at my parents who were happy of this. I was very happy because I didn't meet my sister from a long time and I'm looking forward to see her. The plain left from Bari at 10.00 am and arrived at London at 11.30 am. When I got down from the plain I found my sister that waited for me. I kissed her and we went her home.

COMMENTS

4 marks

There is some organisation – what the ticket was, the reasons why she was happy, the actual trip – and some linking of sentences, e.g. *my parents who were, I was happy because ... and I'm looking ..., When I got down I found ...* .The range of vocabulary and structures is slightly more than adequate, e.g. *immediately , look forward to, It was my sister's present* . However, the story requires a little effort by the reader (*I didn't meet my sister, I'm looking forward to see her*) and there are some errors (which do not obscure the message), e.g. *found my sister, show ... at.*

Question 8: sample answer

> Dear Mary,
> Thank you for the letter, I like it. I'll try to answer your questions. The party was very amusing, and I enjoyed it. I went to a pizzeria, called 'Tarantini al cancello rotto'. In this pizzeria the pizza is very good. Donato, the organizator, was very happy. We first ate pizza, then we ate a good cake. Because we weren't very hungry, we threw cream to each other: a cream war was started. A big piece of cake hit me and I was dirty: my mother was very ungry, when I arrived home.
> The party was very amusing. There were every my class-friends, and I met a beautiful girl. When I returned home, I was very tired. But I was happy.
> Write me soon
> Yours
> Giovanni

COMMENTS

5 marks

A very good attempt, showing confident use of past tense forms, e.g. *we weren't, it hit me, I met* and vocabulary, e.g. *threw, cream war, each other*. Giovanni uses simple linking words appropriately, e.g. *We first ... and then we, Because we ..., we threw cream ..., When I returned home, I ...* . Most mistakes do not make it difficult for the reader to understand, e.g. *ungry* for *angry* and *organizator*. One grammatical error is due to ambition: *There were every my classfriends*, but the meaning is clear.

Paper 2 Listening

Part 1

1 C 2 C 3 C 4 B 5 A 6 B 7 A

Tapescript

Questions 1–7

There are seven questions in this part. For each question there are three pictures and a short recording. Choose the correct picture and put a tick in the box below it.

Example: How does the woman travel to work?
M: Did you buy that car you were interested in?
F: I decided I couldn't afford it and anyway there's nowhere to park near work. I'm going to carry on getting the bus and maybe buy a bike sometime.
M: That's a good idea. Cycling is a very healthy option!

1 Who did the man see yesterday?
M: Do you remember my friend Jane?
F: Yes, she had a boyfriend called Tony, didn't she. I remember he was really tall and had dark hair – his mum worked in the local supermarket.
M: That's right. Well, they're married now. I saw them both at the cinema last night.

2 Where's the computer?
F: Have you been using your new computer?
M: I haven't even taken it out of the box. My new desk hasn't arrived, so I've got nowhere to put it.
F: Can't you use the table in the kitchen?
M: It's too low and anyway I want to work in the bedroom.

3 What did the man have in the restaurant?
F: What did you think of that new restaurant?
M: I didn't like anything on the menu! Nobody told me it was a fish restaurant! I hate fish. The only thing I could have was salad and chips.
F: I thought they did meat as well.
M: Well, they don't.

4 What was stolen on Saturday?
F: ... police have had reports of a couple running from the scene and driving off in a dark green car. The woman was wearing an expensive gold necklace. They were both probably in their late twenties. There is a reward for anybody with information leading to the return of the painting, which is worth at least £50,000.

5 What does the man do?
F: Hello Mark! How's the new job? Are you still enjoying office life?
M: Well, actually I left about a month ago. I decided I wasn't really interested in computers and that I wanted to teach English, so I've got a job in a shop for the moment, and I'm going to start a course next September.

6 What time are they meeting?
M: The film starts at 7.30, so shall we meet at six? We could go for a meal first.
F: Six is a bit early for me. I've got quite a lot to do this afternoon. How about 7.15 outside the cinema? We could always go for something to eat after the film. I think it finishes at about 9.30.
M: OK. I'll see you later.

7 What is the weather like today?
M: ... and if anyone is driving in the area, please take extra care, especially if you're driving on country roads. There have been several reports of trees blown down and there may be heavy rain tomorrow morning. Stay at home in the warm is my advice!

Part 2

8 A   9 B   10 C   11 B   12 C   13 A

Tapescript

Questions 8–13

You will hear someone welcoming a group of visitors to *Ocean Life* sea park. For each question, put a tick in the correct box.

M:
Welcome to *Ocean Life*. It's wonderful to see so many people here today. I'm sure some of you have been here before, but if you haven't, please spare a few minutes before you begin your visit. so that I can tell you something about our sea park. As you probably know, water covers over two thirds of our planet, yet we're only just beginning to explore our oceans. Here at *Ocean Life* we try to re-create parts of this world so that everybody can experience its wonders in the most enjoyable and relaxing way possible. *Ocean Life* is set in fantastic grounds and we advise you to spend several hours wandering around. There are over forty displays, from crabs to penguins to sharks for you to see, as well as plenty of other activities for all the family. We feel that it is better that some sea life such as whales, dolphins and some types of sharks aren't kept in a sea park, because they have better lives in their natural homes. However, although you won't see these creatures here, you will read about them in many of our interesting and educational displays. Education is important, but we know that being entertained while finding things out is equally important, especially for our younger visitors. We do this very successfully through our talks and feeding demonstrations. These occur throughout the day; you'll find information about times in your programme or on the posters just inside the entrance. Our specially trained educational staff can answer any of your questions about the sea, sea life, pollution and conservation. We also encourage school visits, and help parents and teachers by providing information and ideas for use in the classroom both before and after. We invite teachers to come before the visit to discuss anything they are uncertain about, and we offer special rates for education groups throughout the week. *Ocean Life* is also well known for its rescue programmes. We offer care facilities for injured creatures sent to us from different parts of Europe, which we return to their natural homes when they are strong enough. We are also involved in many projects throughout the world, and it is our aim to make sure that our visitors become aware of the problems and dangers that affect sea life. If you want to find out any more about our programmes and to look at ways that you too can help, there are plenty of leaflets at the entrance. Please take one. Thank you very much for listening to me. I'm now very happy to answer any of your questions.

Part 3

14 two/2
15 flight

16 Sunday
17 discount
18 restaurants
19 October

Tapescript

Questions 14–19
You will hear somebody talking about a short break in Barcelona. For each question, fill in the missing information in the numbered space.

F:
... and now on to this month's best short breaks. There's nothing like a long weekend in a foreign city to make you feel good and this month we've found some great breaks in Paris, Madrid, Rome and Venice with (14) breaks ranging from two nights to seven – details of these can be found on our website. But our favourite short break of the month is three nights in Barcelona. The cost (15) of the Barcelona break pays for your flight and your hotel. It also includes a full continental breakfast. Evening meals are not included. You can stay at a hotel of your choice and the hotels (16) range from 2-star to 5-star – there are discounts however, if one of the nights you stay is a Sunday. This applies to all the hotels. Barcelona is a city for art lovers, but we all know how much (17) sightseeing costs can be, so for a very small extra cost this break also offers a discount card that will give you money off (18) many of the city sights. The card also allows you 10% discount in certain restaurants around the city. (19) This Barcelona Break can be enjoyed anytime between the 5th and the 31st of October, although bookings must be made before the end of September. You can book through our website or, if you prefer, you can telephone direct. This is a fantastic offer. Don't miss it!

Part 4

20 B   21 B   22 A   23 B   24 A   25 B

Tapescript

Questions 20–25
Look at the six sentences for this part. You will hear a conversation between a girl, Anna, and a boy, James, about a party. Decide if each sentence is correct or incorrect.
If it is correct, put a tick in the box under A for YES. If it is not correct, put a tick in the box under B for NO.

M: My brother's getting engaged next month.
F: Oh yeah? That sounds like fun. Are they having a big party?
M: I suppose so.
(20) F: You don't sound very excited about it.
M: I'm not.
F: Don't you like his girlfriend?
(21) M: Yeah I do actually. She's quite nice. She makes me laugh. It's just that I'm not keen on family parties. They're always really boring. Everybody sits around and hardly speaks to each other. Either that or somebody has a big argument with somebody else and then doesn't speak to them for years.
(22) F: It's not like that for us. I quite like seeing aunts and uncles I haven't seen for ages and I always have a really good time with my cousins.

M: There's a big age difference between me and my cousins.
(23) They're all about ten years older than me, so we've got nothing to talk about.
F: Well, you might enjoy the party anyway. They'll be lots of food, won't there?
M: I expect so.
(24) F: What about a present? I hope you haven't forgotten about that.
M: Actually I had. I think my mum's got some ideas. I need to talk to her.
F: Well... if you need any help choosing. I'll come with you.
M: Or I could look on the internet. Have you ever bought anything that way?
(25) F: No. I've always been a bit nervous about it.
M: So have I. I always think whatever I buy won't arrive.
F: Well, we could have a look together if you liked.
M: Thanks. That would be great. You can come to the party as well if you want to.
F: Thanks ... but I'm not sure about that!

Paper 3 Speaking

(Suggested language and structures that may be needed to do the tasks.)

Part 2

box of chocolates/sweets; CDs; watches; bowl; plant

look round the shops/on the internet/go shopping
find out what they need/want/like/prefer
make sure they haven't got one

I like the idea of ...
We could either get them ... or ...
Why don't we ... ?

I'm not too keen on ...
That might be a bit boring/dull.

Part 3

Photo 1: queue of traffic/busy streets/feel stressed/not moving/ slow journey/create pollution/people crossing the street
Photo 2: ride a bike/quiet street/no cars/shopping street/better for the environment/avoid the queues/could be dangerous

Part 4

bike/bicycle, car, train, underground, tram, motorbike, moped, bus, (aero)plane, boat, ferry

I like travelling by (car) because it's relaxing/fast/cheap/ comfortable/you can see a lot.
I hate travelling (on the bus) because it's slow/crowded/ expensive/dirty/noisy/uncomfortable/dangerous.

I prefer to travel by (underground) because it's cheaper/ more convenient/more regular than ...
(trains) aren't as fast/comfortable/as ...

Test 2

Paper 1 Reading and Writing

Reading

Part 1

1 A   2 C   3 B   4 B   5 C

Part 2

(The key words from each person are given opposite the key words from the answers.)

6 B

Sarah	The Lost Gold
enjoys films that scare her ——	frightening film
well made ————	excellent acting and a clever story
doesn't like to be able to guess what's going to happen	You'll never guess the ending

7 D

Maria	Lonely Lives
serious films … about people and relationships	a lonely boy who becomes friends with a lonely man
stories that take place the past	most of the film happens in in the 1960s

8 G

Simon	The Search
fun films that entertain/ likes to laugh	fast action and great comedy
easy to understand/guess what's going to happen	a simple story

9 F

Juan	My Father
films that make him think ——	keep you guessing
keen on sport ————	baseball/the best player/ the team

10 A

Sally	Going Home
crime stories ————	she has been kidnapped
films that surprise ————	shock ending

Part 3

11 **A Correct.** *Over half those taking Learn Now courses* do more than one course (l.5).

12 **B Incorrect.** *Learn Now is perfect for anyone who hasn't been successful with traditional ways of learning* (l.9), not just those who have done well at school.

13 **A Correct.** You study only *what you want to learn when you want to learn it* (l.10).

14 **B Incorrect.** Testing is not an important part because *you don't have to take any exams* (l.12).

15 **A Correct.** Some companies use Learn Now *as part of their staff development* (l.15).

16 **B Incorrect.** You don't need basic skills, in fact *you don't need experience or knowledge for any of our courses* (l.22).

17 **B Incorrect.** You don't need to learn at a centre because you *can learn by distance learning at home or work* (l.24).

18 **A Correct.** As soon as you contact Learn Now they *will get you started without delay* (l.28).

19 **B Incorrect.** You do not need to attend regularly because *you just book in whenever you want to* (l.30).

20 **B Incorrect.** You do not need to go to a centre at least once because they *can organise everything by telephone or e-mail* (l.31).

Part 4

(The first answer given is always the correct one.)

21 **B** The text explains that human beings are used to sleeping at night, asks if working at night is natural, and says how night work can damage your health and cause accidents.
A x The writer mentions *doing something important at work* (1.14), but not the importance of work in general.
C x The writer says that working at night means changing your way of life but doesn't suggest people do so.
D x The writer says that people need different amounts of sleep but doesn't say they need to sleep more.

22 **D** *more and more jobs need to be done at night* (l.4); hotels, companies, supermarkets and emergency services are mentioned.
A The writer says that *few people can work well at night* (l.8) but not that they refuse to.
B It seems it is harder than working during the day.
C Working conditions aren't mentioned.

23 **B** *we cannot easily change our sleeping habits* (l.8).
A *You're either a 'short sleeper' or a 'long sleeper'* (l.10).
C The worst part of the day for being awake is between 2 a.m. and 4 a.m.
D *others need as many as eleven hours* (l.10), but the writer doesn't mention people needing more than that.

24 **B** The writer believes a 24-hour society will remain (l.18).
A The writer says that more jobs are done at night but not that fewer people will work during the day.
C The writer says that more services are 24 hour.
D Working hours aren't mentioned.

25 **C** The article focuses on a new 24-hour society but says we will *never be able to do things the other way round* (l.17).
A The writer says that too little sleep is bad for you but doesn't talk about the benefits.
B The relationship between the amount of sleep and amount of work isn't discussed.
D There is no mention of any jobs being lonely.

Part 5

26 A
whether … or shows a contrast. B, C and D do not go with *or*.

27 B
A, C and D are not followed by *to*.

28 A
People who live is the correct defining relative clause. B, C and D do not fit.

29 C
along means 'by the side of'. A, B and D have the wrong meaning here.

30 B
gives you the benefit of means 'gives you the good things about'. A, C and D have the wrong meaning here.

31 C
A and D have the wrong meaning here; B should be *find out about*.

32 A
more than …ever is the correct comparison. B, C and D have the wrong meaning here.

33 B
A, C and D are not about place.

34 D
A and C aren't used for advice; B needs 'to'.

35 B
A and C should be 'stay/keep away from'; D needs another verb after *let*.

Writing

Part 1

1 Meat isn't **as good** for you as fish.
2 You **can buy snacks** in the café.
3 He's really **good at** cooking.
4 There aren't very **many** good restaurants in this area.
5 Everybody **should/ought to eat** plenty of fruit and vegetables.

Part 2

Question 6: sample answer

> Dear Paul,
> I'm sorry. I forgot your's birthday. I'm very stupid but I had a lots of homework to do. What about going to eat something? I should you to answer yes because I have also a program for have fun. I'm free only Saturday if you want to do this program call me friday. See you soon
> Your
> Alessandro

COMMENTS
4 marks
Although all content elements are covered, Alessandro has written 60 words (the word limit is 45) and part of his message is unclear and unnecessary – he only had to suggest taking Paul out for a meal.

Part 3

Question 7: sample answer

> I was surprised when I arrived at the bus stop. There was man who was calling me. He said: 'Vincenzo!!! Come here!!'. I walked and I stopped in front of him. He was my friend Roberto! 'Roberto', I said 'Where are you! I've been calling you for three years!' His face changed rapidly. 'My wife died and I went to work in America since 2000.' The bus driver was waiting us. 'Do you want to come up?' he said 'No', I said. After I asked 'Roberto, do you want to come to my house? We can talk about school …' I found a friend. That was a very beautiful day.

COMMENTS
5 marks
A very good attempt, showing confident and ambitious use of language. There is a good range of structures and vocabulary, e.g. *a man who was, I've been calling you for..., I found a friend, changed rapidly*. It is coherent and it reads well. There are a few errors, e.g. *Where are you, I went to work ... since 2000, was waiting us*, but the meaning is clear and the reader does not have to make an effort to understand.

Question 8: sample answer

> Dear Jane,
> How are you? I hope you stay well. Here the weather is too cold so For Me is very difficult to practice My favourites hobbies.
> What's the weather do in your country?
> I think that It's no import to you because you hobby is all cover.
> Now I like to go to swim and when the weather is quite good I like run as you know.
> Last weekend I went to sky in a country Near my place.
> In last period I like too go on bike with My friend, Is fantastic to watch the sea on winter but it's very cold.
> Now I had made 100 words, more or less, so I can said:
> bye bye

COMMENTS
2 marks
This is an inadequate attempt. The language is repetitive, e.g. *I like to go, I like run, I like too go on bike*. There is an insufficient range of structures and vocabulary and a lot of errors, e.g. *stay well, what's the weather do, it's no import, your hobby is all cover, in last period*, some of which make the message difficult to understand. There is little attempt to answer the second question, and the last sentence is irrelevant.

Paper 2 Listening

Part 1

1 B   2 A   3 C   4 B   5 A   6 B   7 B

Tapescript

Questions 1–7
There are seven questions in this part. For each question there are three pictures and a short recording. Choose the correct picture and put a tick in the box below it.

Example: How does the woman travel to work?
M: Did you buy that car you were interested in?
F: I decided I couldn't afford it and anyway there's nowhere to park near work. I'm going to carry on getting the bus and maybe buy a bike sometime.
M: That's a good idea. Cycling is a very healthy option!

1 How did the accident happen?
M: ... and anyone travelling in the area today should expect traffic jams after an accident involving a lorry that lost control and crashed through a shop window in Maine Street. Nobody was hurt, but the driver is in shock and has been unable to tell the police what happened yet. Witnesses have said however, he was trying to avoid a cyclist although no cyclists have come forward yet.

2 What pet are they going to buy?
M: I think we should get a pet. What do you think?
F: A dog would be nice, or a cat maybe?
M: Dogs need a lot of looking after and I'm not keen on cats. They make me sneeze. I've always liked the idea of tropical fish.
F: Well they need almost as much looking after as dogs, but they look nice, so OK.

3 Where is the mobile phone?
F: Jack, have you seen my mobile? I'm sure I left it on the table.
M: You did. I picked it up and put it in your bag – the one hanging on the back of the chair. Have you looked?
F: No I haven't .... Yes, it's still here. Thanks.

4 When are they going to celebrate the end of their exams?
M: My last exam's on the 15th. What about you? Shall we go out and celebrate?
F: Yeah. I'd love to. My last one's on the 16th.
M: Well, we could go out on the 17th then.
F: Actually, I think I'd like to go out straight after my last exam. We could go for something to eat.

5 What does Alison's new boyfriend look like?
F: Have you met Alison's new boyfriend?
M: I think so. He's quite short and he's got blond hair.
F: That was Jack. He was the last one! They haven't been together for ages. Mike's got dark hair and he's much taller.

6 Where has Sally been?
M: Sally! Where have you been? I waited at the café for ages! We were supposed to meet there hours ago.
F: Sorry, Mark. Somebody from work had an accident and had to go to hospital. She was really worried about her son so I offered to pick him up from school. I tried to call you, but your phone was switched off.

7 What can you buy during the interval?
F: Ladies and gentlemen ... may I remind you that there will be an interval of twenty minutes during which there will be cold drinks and light snacks , including sandwiches and cakes, on sale at the bar. We regret to say that tea and coffee and hot food are not available this evening. Would you please now take your seats. The play is about to begin.

Part 2

8 C   9 B   10 C   11 A   12 A   13 B

Tapescript

Questions 8–13
You will hear someone reviewing a music night. For each question, put a tick in the correct box.

M:
The Old Oak in Cambridge Road is famous in the area for its excellent food and great family atmosphere especially at Sunday lunchtimes, but now the pub has come up with a great new idea. Don't worry, Sunday lunchtimes won't end, but now the pub has decided to take an interest in music too. They've come up with a great idea to encourage local bands and (8) to attract young people and on Saturday 29th July, they held what they hope will be the first of many live music nights. The idea is to give local bands a great place to perform. Unlike in some places, the bands at the Old Oak are paid! They are also (9) offered free practice time and space in the pub three weeks before they are booked to play. Saturday's show had local rock band *Living World*. The band, who have been playing together for about a year now, were joined last month by Sally Mallet, who some of you may have heard of. She was the singer of *The* (10) *Squares*, an all-girl band also local to the area. Sally's rich voice has really made a difference to the previously all-male *Living World*. On Saturday, there was a great atmosphere in the pub with everyone really enjoying the music. The band was very lively and exciting to watch and they played some excellent sounds. *Happy World* was the most popular song, and the band (11) managed to carry on playing even when part of their equipment exploded on stage! Nobody was hurt and things soon got back to normal! The place wasn't crowded, but (12) most of *Living World*'s student fans are away at the moment. However, those who hadn't left the area came and enjoyed the evening's entertainment and were joined by quite a few locals as well. Everybody stayed right to the end and had a great time. And now the band has fans who hadn't heard of them before! (13) Bands interested in playing at the Old Oak should send a demonstration tape to the pub direct, but please remember that bands can only play if at least two of their members are local. However, past success isn't important. You can find out more details by contacting Mike at the Old Oak.

Part 3

14 Hapston
15 Friday
16 midday/twelve/12
17 dessert
18 drink
19 two/2

Tapescript

Questions 14–19
You will hear somebody on the radio talking about a restaurant. For each question, fill in the missing information in the numbered space.

F:
If you want to eat out this weekend and you're not sure where to go, try the new Rooftop Restaurant. It's just outside town
(14) in Hapston Village. That's H-A-P-S-T-O-N. You'll find it at the end of Market Street, which is right next to the river. I was very lucky to be invited to last Tuesday's pre-opening private dinner, but it
(15) opens to the public on 18th October – that's this Friday. The food is European, combining English, French and Italian styles, and I had an excellent three-course meal, chosen from the menu. I went in the evening, but I'll probably try lunchtime next time.
(16) The restaurant is open every day for lunch. It opens at midday and closes again at three. There's a fixed two-course menu –
(17) if you want dessert, you pay a bit more. On Sundays, you can have a traditional Sunday lunch for the same price. The evening meals begin at seven and the last meal can be ordered at ten. The average three-course meal, such as the one I had, is very
(18) reasonable, and until the end of October, the price includes a drink. The restaurant has lovely views across the river and the best seats are of course, by the window, but you'll be lucky if you get one of those! In any case you should book two or three days before, as I have a feeling this restaurant is going to be very popular! The restaurant is happy to take group bookings for
(19) specific celebrations provided they are booked two weeks before. It's not a large restaurant, so the maximum they'll take in a group is twenty.

Part 4

20 A   21 B   22 A   23 A   24 B   25 B

Tapescript

Questions 20–25
Look at the six sentences for this part. You will hear a conversation between a girl, Meg, and a boy, David, about their plans for the future. Decide if each sentence is correct or incorrect. If it is correct, put a tick in the box under A for YES. If it is not correct, put a tick in the box under B for NO.

F: I'm thinking of taking a year off when I finish my exams. I don't want to go straight to university.
(20) M: I wouldn't do that if I were you. It could be a big mistake.
F: What do you mean? Why?
M: Well, if you get a good job, for example, you might get so used to the money, you won't want to go back to being a poor student.
(21) F: Actually that's not what I want to do. I want to travel abroad.
M: How can you afford it?
F: I thought I'd work as a volunteer. Some organisations pay your travel and you work for nothing. That would be great.
M: What would you do?
F: Work in a school, maybe, or on a farm.
M: How would that help you with the degree you want to do?
F: Well. I'm going to do French and Spanish, aren't I? I could go
(22) to South America, or somewhere. My Spanish would really improve if I lived there. But anyway, a gap year isn't just about getting something that helps you with your course, it's about getting experience of life!
(23) M: You don't have to go abroad for that.
F: That's true, but I like travelling! I want to see places all over the world, and this would be a good opportunity.
M: You might be lonely! You've never been travelling on your own.

(24) F: I haven't been to many places at all, but that's why I'd like to go now.
M: If I were you, I'd rather get my course over and then go travelling after that. Then I wouldn't have to worry about rushing back to go to college. I could stay away for as long as I liked.
(25) F: Yeah. I see what you mean, but I feel like I need a break from study and exams now.
M: Well, if you change your mind let me know! We'll start planning a trip abroad for three years' time! I've always fancied a trip to China.

Paper 3 Speaking

Part 2

(Suggested lamguage and structures that may be needed to do the tasks.)

cows/animals: noisy/smelly/dirty
car park: noisy/loud/dirty/dangerous
showers: busy/people going in and out/dustbins/smelly
river/stream: quiet/relaxing/plenty of space
tree: shade/shady/quiet

I don't think … would be very nice because …
I don't think we should …
It could/might be a bit … there.
It might be nice …
I (don't) like the idea of …

Part 3

Photo 1: at a nightclub/listen to music/have fun
celebrate something/a night out with friends
Photo 2: two couples/go for/have a quiet meal/something to eat/a few friends/have a chat

Part 4

Entertainment: sport, cinema, eating out, bowling, clubs and discos, shopping, listen to music, visit friends, watch videos

I sometimes/occasionally/often/always …
I like … I prefer … I'm really interested in …
I'm not keen on … I don't really like …

Test 3

Paper 1 Reading and Writing

Reading

Part 1

1 B   2 A   3 C   4 A   5 C

Part 2

(The key words from each person are given opposite the key words from the answers.)

6 E

Maria	La Villa
student	reasonably priced
in the centre	central part
bars and clubs	cafés/nightlife
doesn't want to spend much on food	all meals are included in the price

7 A

Stefan	Hotel Inn
business trip/hire a room for meetings	facilities for conferences
eat at the hotel	choice of three restaurants
get to and from the airport easily	easy to reach … the airport

8 D

Eleni	Hotel Etoile
shopping/close to the shops	within walking distance of the best stores
leisure facilities	heated swimming pool, steam room and gym

9 G

Kathryn and Klaus	Hotel Bel Air
quiet part	peaceful part
prefer the hotel to organise trips	the hotel will arrange group sightseeing

10 C

Paolo	The Trocadero
studying French painting	perfect for art lovers/ close to … galleries
chance to meet other people	a bar where guests can socialise

Part 3

11 **A Correct.** Advice is available on open days *when new pupils … can come to the centre* (l.10).

12 **A Correct.** The number of pupils learning an instrument in a small group is *three or four pupils* (l.18).

13 **B Incorrect.** Only … *pupils who have some experience* can be taught their instrument on their own (l.22).

14 **B Incorrect.** Lessons do not take place at the same school as they *are available in many schools* (l.25).

15 **A Correct.** It is possible to have a lesson at the weekend because *arrangements can be made … for lessons on Saturday afternoons* (l.28).

16 **B Incorrect.** Parents should not *buy an instrument until they are told that a place is available* (l.35).

17 **A Correct.** Singing helps students to improve other skills such as *communication, and … provides good training for acting too* (l.43).

18 **B Incorrect.** Students are not expected to but they *can choose to take exams* (l.46).

19 **B Incorrect.** Not only eight children can go to 'Musical Youth' classes because there are *groups of about 18 children* (l.56).

20 **A Correct.** Parents can join in because they *are encouraged to sit with their child and help them with the activities* (l.58).

Part 4

(The first answer given is always the correct one.)

21 **D** She says the brain *needs to be cared for* (l.2) and suggests ways of improving it.
  A x She says *nobody really understands everything about it* (l.1) and doesn't talk about how it works.
  B x She only says that *many people think their brain will slow down* (l.6).
  C x She gives examples of her own experiences but doesn't say that she is clever.

22 **B** The writer is learning Spanish (l.14).
  A Computers are mentioned (l.16) but we don't know if she has one.
  C She gives shopping as an example (l.11) but doesn't say if she likes it.
  D This is an example of how to improve your mind (l.13) but we don't know if she enjoys travelling.

23 **A** *Just like our bodies, it needs to be cared for …* (l.2).
  B There is no comment about how much medical research is done.
  C Many people think this (l.6), but it isn't necessarily true.
  D She doesn't say this, she only suggests that you can improve both body and mind (l.6).

24 **A** *I've found I can improve my memory* (l.7).
  B She talks about remembering dates (l.11) but doesn't compare remembering numbers and objects.
  C It has improved (l.7).
  D She uses birthday cards only as an example (l.10).

25 **A** She gives examples in paragraphs 2 and 3.
  B She doesn't talk about the latest research.
  C She talks about how to improve memory, not about how powerful it is.
  D She doesn't discuss things that you've already forgotten.

Part 5

26 D

so many is positive; A is negative and B and C cannot go before *many*.

27 B

A, C and D do not follow the verb *depend*.

28 A

B, C and D do not have the right meaning.

29 C

A doesn't make sense here; B and D are followed by 'of + -ing'.

30 D

A, B and C do not have the right meaning.

31 A

even means that this is something unexpected.
B, C and D have the wrong meaning.

32 B

by means 'next to'; D must be followed by 'to'; A and C have the wrong meaning.

33 B

A, C and D do not make a phrase with *boat*.

34 D

spend time means 'pass time'; A, B and C have the wrong meaning here.

35 C

A, B and D cannot follow *love* here.

Writing

Part 1

1 Going on holiday isn't as **exciting as** living abroad.
2 You can't work in some countries **unless** you have a visa.
3 My German improved as **soon as** I started living there.
4 It isn't **easy** travelling alone in a foreign country.
5 He isn't old **enough** to work abroad.

Part 2

Question 6: sample answer

> Hi Anna,
> On Saturday night I'll having a birthday party at my house and I want to invite you. You can arrive in Bari with a train and if you want I can pick you up from the station. If you want you can stay with me for a few days.
> See you soon,
> Louis

COMMENTS

5 marks

All parts of the question are covered appropriately. The error in the first sentence (*I'll having*) does not make the message difficult to understand.

Part 3

Question 7: sample answer

> Dear Nick,
> thanks for your letter. I'm going to answer to your questions. During weekends, I spend time with my friends. At eight p.m., we meet in a pinewood, that is situated in front of my house.

> Then we go to a pub where we eat pizza and we drink coke. Some of my friends buy a bottle of beer but I really hate it. The thing I like doing best is going to the disco. There we dance, shout and ... It's wonderful!! But this weekend is different. I have to study for a classwork and I can't go out with my friends. I am very sad! By the way I really enjoy your letter and I hope you'll write to me soon. Love
> Rossella

COMMENTS

5 marks

This is a very good attempt which requires no effort by the reader. It is well organised, e.g. *at eight o'clock ... then we go ... there we dance … But this weekend …*. There is a good range of structures and vocabulary, e.g. *situated, a pub where we eat, The thing I like … is …*. Errors are present, e.g. *answer to your questions, study for a classwork*, but they are minor.

Question 8: sample answer

> THE RAINY DAY
> When in the morning I was standing up the bed, the cool air in the room has stopped my legs. 'Another rainy day' - mouth has pronounced desperately and sadly. I was going in the kitchen, I've prepared the coffee machine and I've continued watching rain out the window with empty eyes. I've drunk my coffee thinking hard working day that was waiting for me, the noise of the traffic, the screams of the boss, the looks of the ugly girls. When I've finished my coffee, my legs moved themselves to my bed, my hands saluted the world and I took another sleep.

COMMENTS

3 marks

This answer is very ambitious but has problems. The story is well organised and the errors with structures do not generally make it difficult to understand, e.g. *I was going in the kitchen, I've drunk my coffee*. The writer has used a wide range of vocabulary, e.g. *desperately, sadly, empty eyes, screams*. However, some words and phrases are used incorrectly and make the meaning unclear, e.g. *standing up the bed, stopped my legs, saluted*. Parts of the story require more than a little effort by the reader.

Paper 2 Listening

Part 1

1 B 2 B 3 B 4 A 5 B 6 C 7 C

Tapescript

Questions 1–7

There are seven questions in this part. For each question there are three pictures and a short recording. Choose the correct picture and put a tick in the box below it.

Example: How does the woman travel to work?
M: Did you buy that car you were interested in?
F: I decided I couldn't afford it and anyway there's nowhere to park near work. I'm going to carry on getting the bus and maybe buy a bike sometime.
M: That's a good idea. Cycling is a very healthy option!

113

1 What time will the train arrive at the station?
Passengers waiting for the ten o'clock train are advised that this is running thirty minutes late . This is due to strong winds which blew a tree onto the line at three o'clock this morning. We apologise for the delay.

2 What is the woman going to do on holiday?
F: We're going to France for a couple of weeks in September, tickets are a bit cheaper then.
M: Are you staying on the coast or are you going to visit lots of different places?
F: Well, the village we're hoping to stay in isn't far from the coast , it's probably only about a thirty minute drive, but we thought we'd leave the car behind and go walking instead of going to the beach.
M: Sounds very healthy.

3 What is the guest going to talk about?
... My next guest began his career as a singer, and only moved into acting when he reached his forties. His greatest film is probably *Long Journey*, which came out on video last year. He has since written about his exciting and full life in the book *Making it Happen* and that is what he'll tell us about tonight . Ladies and Gentlemen would you please welcome Charles Price ...

4 Where did the man go last night?
F: I didn't see you at the party last night.
M: The car didn't start. We didn't feel like getting a bus all that way, so we went for a meal instead. We saw a couple of other friends there. They'd been to the new cinema that's just opened in town. We're thinking of going next weekend. Do you want to come?

5 Where does Anna live now?
M: Hi Anna. I haven't seen you for a long time. Are you still living in that flat by the park?
F: I was until about two weeks ago. I got fed up with sharing and moved out. I'm back at mum and dad's house for now , but I'm planning to buy one of those new flats they've built by the river – maybe on the ground floor so I can have a garden.

6 What does the man's teacher look like?
F: Are you still doing keep fit classes? I haven't seen you there for ages.
M: I moved to a different class. I wasn't keen on the teacher at the old one. I've got Chris now.
F: Chris? Is he the one with short dark hair? He always wears a baseball cap.
M: You're thinking of somebody else. Chris has got dark hair, but it's long and he ties it back. He does Tuesday and Thursday evenings.

7 Where is the letter?
F: Could you do me a favour and post a letter?
M: Sure. Is it on your desk?
F: It's under a pile of papers, next to the computer. There's a letter-box at the end of the street. Do you know the one I mean?
M: Yeah. I'm going that way anyway.

Part 2

8 C   9 A   10 B   11 A   12 B   13 C

Tapescript

Questions 8–13
You will hear an interview with a writer. For each question, put a tick in the correct box.

F: Today writer Jack Spears is going to tell us about his writing day. Jack, some people think that writers write when they feel like it and that it is more like a hobby than a job. Would you agree?
M: Definitely not. Although it's only recently that writing has become my only job, I've never seen it as a hobby.
(8) Even when I was a child, I took my stories very seriously. When I was a teacher, I used to start writing at about 9 o'clock in the evening, and go on until about one or two in the morning.
F: And what about now?
(9) M: I get up at seven in the morning six days a week and go for a 30-minute run. On Sundays I go swimming. Sitting at a computer is so unhealthy I think all writers should at least go for a walk during their working day.
F: When do you start writing?
M: At about 9 o'clock. I work through until lunchtime, about midday, although sometimes it's closer to one, and have a short break for something to eat.
(10) F: Do you ever eat while you are working?
M: Sometimes I'd like to, but it's my rule not to. I think it's important to go somewhere else and concentrate on your food.
(11) F: Where do you work?
M: I have my own office , but in fact, my wife is at work and my children are at school all day, so I could work anywhere in the house if I wanted to, even on the kitchen table. But then I'd have to clear everything away at the end of the day and I wouldn't like that.
F: Do you write after lunch?
M: I usually deal with post and e-mails and then write again in the evening.
(12) F: How long does it take you to write a novel?
M: It usually takes about six months to write it for the first time. I then put it away for a month and do other things, such as writing short stories. After that, I start re-writing and that can take another six or seven months.
(13) F: How do you feel when you've finished? Do you take a break from writing?
M: No, I don't. I carry on with my next project. I may decide to go away for a while, with the family, but I always take work with me. It may be another novel, or it may be a collection of short stories, or perhaps a magazine article.
F: How do your family feel about that?
M: They don't mind. They're used to me by now.

Part 3

14 Saturday
15 first floor
16 sportswear
17 canteen
18 two forty-five/2.45
19 bookshop

Tapescript

Questions 14–19
You will hear somebody talking about a fashion show.
For each question, fill in the missing information in the numbered space.

F:
Next month, students from the fashion department at Iffley College will be holding an exciting event to collect money for children. They are putting on a fashion show which will take
(14) place on Saturday 25th June. The show will be held in the new
(15) drama studio on the first floor of the college. Students themselves will be modelling the clothes, which have been given to them by various well-known stores in the area. There will be a range of clothes from high street store to designer boutique. Something for everyone. The show starts at 11.30 am
(16) and begins with a presentation of men's fashion, which will include sportswear. There will be a short break for lunch at
(17) 12.30 when a cold buffet will be served in the canteen, the cost of which is included in the price of the ticket. The show will continue at 1.30 with women's fashion, which will include both winter and summer wear. The show will end at
(18) 2.45 with a presentation of the students' own designs. Come and support your local college and help children in need at the same time. It'll be a fun day out! You can buy tickets for the show on the college website, or over the phone.
(19) You can also get them at the college bookshop, which is on the ground floor next to the admissions office. Full details of prices and where the clothes are available from will appear on your programme or you can find them on the college website.

Part 4

20 A   21 A   22 B   23 B   24 B   25 B

Tapescript

Questions 20–25
Look at the six sentences for this part. You will hear a conversation between a girl, Sarah, and a boy, Thomas, about moving abroad. Decide if each sentence is correct or incorrect. If it is correct, put a tick in the box under A for YES. If it is not correct, put a tick in the box under B for NO.

M: I hear you're moving abroad.
F: That's right. We're going to live in Spain.
M: That sounds brilliant. I love Spain.
(20) F: Yeah I really like Spain too, but I'm a bit nervous about going to live abroad.
M: I would be too. It must be hard to leave your friends and everything.
F: Yeah. I'm going to really miss everybody.
(21) M: Well, it's not too far. I'm sure they'll visit you. I definitely will.
F: Good. I hope you do.
(22) M: Where are you going? Have you got a house?
F: We're going to rent somewhere first. It's in the south right near the coast. The sea is only about twenty minutes away.
M: Fantastic.
F: And then in a couple of months we're going to buy somewhere.
M Have your parents got jobs out there?

F: Yeah.
M: Is that why you're going?
(23) F: Not really. They've always dreamed about living abroad. They thought they couldn't go when me and my brother were young and at school, but now we're at college they think it's OK.
M: So you're going to college in Spain?
(24) F: Yeah. But my brother's going to stay where he is, in London. He's older than me.
M: Do you speak any Spanish?
F: A bit. I'm doing a course at the moment and we're not going for a couple of months yet.
(25) M: So you should be quite good by then.
F: I don't know about that. I think I'll need a bit more time.
M: You'll be all right once you get there.
F: Maybe after a couple of months.
M: It doesn't take long to learn a language when you live somewhere. Maybe I should start learning too if I'm going to visit you!

Paper 3 Speaking

(Suggested language and structures that may be needed to do the tasks.)

Part 2

go walking: in the countryside/fresh air/beautiful scenery
go jogging: in the park/early in the morning/train for a marathon
go swimming: excellent exercise for your whole body/relaxing
play tennis/badminton: play with friends/have fun
do aerobics/yoga/gymnastics: join a class/meet people/regular exercise

... is fun/convenient/good for you/relaxing
It's nice to go to/see/play ...
It's better/healthier to ... than ...

Part 3

Photo 1: in the country/cottage/peaceful/scenery/birds and animals/clean air
Photo 2: in the city/blocks of flats/busy/noisy/crowded/traffic/polluted air

Part 4

Places: village/town/city/near the sea/on the coast/in the mountains/in the north/south/east/west

I live in a ... . It's in ... and it's ...
It's a small/big/friendly/unfriendly place.
I like the people/atmosphere/shops/entertainment/facilities.

I don't like the traffic/noise/rubbish/pollution.
There's nothing/lots to do.

Test 4

Paper 1 Reading and Writing

Reading

Part 1

1 B   2 B   3 A   4 C   5 A

Part 2

(The key words from each person are given opposite the key words from the answers.)

6 C

Hannah	Sun and Surf!
unfit	try diving, soak up the sun
try different sports	learn to windsurf/try diving

7 D

Alberto	Voyages of Discovery
doesn't want to go to the beach	seven-night cruise/stay on board
opportunities to relax	life slows down/read … do absolutely nothing
visit more than one country	wake up in different countries

8 G

Charlotte	Real Adventure
sea life	watching whales and dolphins
explore underwater	under the sea
other experienced divers	not for beginners/ our skilled crew

9 A

Sue	Desert Island Dream
somewhere hot	near the sea/beautiful beaches
stay in one place	tiny island
do a variety of things/ local area	beaches/giant turtles/ rainforest/food markets/cruise

10 E

Simone and Pedro	Explore the countryside
travel around on interesting forms of transport	canal boat hire
enjoy sightseeing and the countryside	float past woods, fields, pretty villages and historic towns … finest … scenery
explore one country	experience England

Part 3

11   **B Incorrect.** You are not given an identity card as soon as you join because it *takes a few days to make* (l.6).

12   **B Incorrect.** Other people cannot use your membership card because it *is for your use only* (l.9).

13   **B Incorrect.** A programme is organised by a skilled instructor *two or three weeks after you have joined* (l.17).

14   **A Correct.** You must wear certain kinds of clothes including *sportswear and trainers … while exercising* (l.24).

15   **A Correct.** You must take *a small towel into the gymnasium* (l.26).

16   **B Incorrect.** You cannot spend as long as you like on all the equipment because they ask you to *respect other members by only spending 20 minutes on each piece of equipment* (l.30).

17   **A Correct.** Staff are always available to answer your questions because there are *experienced staff in the gymnasiums at all times who will help you … and answer your questions* (l.32).

18   **B Incorrect.** You cannot leave personal items at the gymnasium for 24 hours because *belongings which are found either in a locker or anywhere else overnight will be removed* (l.41).

19   **A Correct.** Drinks are free but you can buy *cold snacks including sandwiches and a range of delicious salads at a very low cost* (l.49).

20   **B Incorrect.** You should not make complaints to the receptionist because *the suggestion box and forms can be found at reception* (l.54).

Part 4

(The first answer given is always the correct one.)

21   **B** Paragraph 2 is about how she found the class and paragraph 3 describes the first class.
A x   This is not the main purpose of the text.
C x   She gives reasons (l.17–18) but this is not the main purpose.
D x   This is not the main purpose.

22   **B** She gives various reasons (l.17–18).
A x   We don't know if she is good.
C x   The dance teacher played *western pop songs* (l.14) but we don't know if the writer normally likes listening to pop music.
D x   She is fitter (l.17) but her main interest is dancing.

23   **A** She became less confident as she became older (l.3).
B x   This isn't known.
C x   She has made friends at the dance class (l.18) but we don't know if she likes meeting people generally.
D x   She was nervous at the first dance class (l.9) but as a child she enjoyed discos, etc. (l.1).

24   **A** *We soon all caught her energy and enthusiasm* (l.12).
B x   *Everyone was really friendly* (l.10).
C x   The writer says the teacher looked fantastic (l.12), but we don't know what the others thought.
D x   They followed the moves (l.14), they didn't discuss them.

25   **C** *Everyone was really friendly* (l.10) and the teacher has *energy and enthusiasm* (l.13).
A x   She wasn't matched with a partner.
B x   The class teaches Indian dancing only not Latin American.
D x   She wanted a class where she didn't need a partner (l.4–5, 7).

Part 5

26 **B**

A should be 'not … anything at all'; C does not go with *at all*; D is for people.

27 **C**

A, B and D have the wrong meaning here.

28 **D**

A would be followed by 'to'; B has the wrong meaning here; C would be followed by 'of'.

29 **D**

own emphasises *your*. A, B and C have the wrong meanings here.

30 **A**

Nowadays means 'at this time'. B and C have the wrong meaning and D has the wrong tense *are written*.

31 **C**

The correct phrase is *talk to* (people). B and D do not follow the verb *talk*. A, *talk at*, has the wrong meaning.

32 **A**

B, C and D do not follow 'a'.

33 **D**

A, B and C are not followed by 'to'.

34 **A**

The correct phrase is 'tell a lie'.
B, C and D have the wrong meaning.

35 **B**

A, C and D do not replace *realising*.

Writing

Part 1

1 If I were you **I would/I'd** switch off the TV and do something more interesting.
2 I used **to love** watching cartoons when I was a child.
3 I like watching films **more/better than** watching documentaries.
4 They **made** that programme in America.
5 I get **bored** by games shows.

Part 2

Question 6: sample answer

> Dear Mary,
> I want to thanks you for the invitation. I'm arrive there on Friday at 11:15 o'clock. When I am there I hope to go in the city to do shopping and see something new.
> Kiss Kiss
> Elizabeth

COMMENTS

5 marks

All three parts to the question are clearly communicated. There are a number of errors (*thanks you, I'm arrive, go in the city, 11:15 o'clock*) but the message is always clear.

Part 3

Question 7: sample answer

> Dear Tom,
> thank you for the letter. Now I answer to you how is my house and where I live. Now I living in a flat in Bari near to a park. I live with my grandmother and with her dog: Cookie, a nice boxer. My family stay in my old town Palo del Calle. About my home I like the terrace because it is covered and when came a friends from school we can play in football or volleyball.
> Today I go to sleep at 23:30 because I have a lot to study.
> By by see you soon
> Giuseppe

COMMENTS

4 marks

This is a more than adequate attempt. There are a number of errors but they do not cause problems for the reader, e.g. *answer to you, how is my house, came a friends*. There is some attempt at organisation and at linking sentences, e.g. *About my home … because … and when …* and some range of vocabulary, e.g. *flat, boxer, old town, terrace, volleyball*.

Question 8: sample answer

> I opened the door very slowly. In my room there was my dog on my bed and my little sister played with my computer. I was very angry because I don't wish that someone in generally come in my room. I hate that my sister use my things and is unthinkable that my dog stay on my bed. From that day I decided to close my room with a key and only to my mother is allowed to entry because she has to do her housework. I hope that she don't read my diary because my privacy is very important.

COMMENTS

5 marks

A very good attempt, showing confident and ambitious use of language. There are a wide range of structures and vocabulary, e.g. *From that day I decided, only (to) my mother is allowed , I hope that, unthinkable, housework, privacy*. Errors are present but they are minor and do not require effort by the reader, e.g. *allowed to entry, she don't*.

Paper 2 Listening

Part 1

1 A   2 B   3 C   4 B   5 C   6 A   7 F

Tapescript

Questions 1–7

There are seven questions in t[...]
are three pictures and a sho[...]
picture and put a tick in th[...]

Example: How does the [...]
M: Did you buy that c[...]
F: I decided I couldn'[...]
park near work. I'm[...]
maybe buy a bik[...]
M: That's a goo[...]

117

1 What is the woman going to read on the plane?
M: Did you bring a book for the journey?
F: No, I forgot. I could buy some magazines at the airport.
M: You can borrow my book if you like. I'll probably read the paper on the plane.
F: Great! Thanks.

2 What will Mr Brown find at the desk?
... If there is a Mr Robert Brown in the store would he please come to the customer services desk as soon as possible where there is an urgent telephone message waiting for him from his wife. The customer service desk is next to electrical goods. Thank you.

3 Where is the hotel?
M: Where are we? I thought we'd be at the hotel by now.
F: It's OK. We're nearly there. Look, there's the sign for the village. We should come to a bridge in a minute. We go over the bridge and the hotel is just on the left after that. There's a shop opposite.
M: Right. I can see the bridge now.

4 How did the woman hear from James?
M: Have you heard from James? He must have arrived in Australia by now! He promised to send me a postcard.
F: He gave me a quick call yesterday. Didn't you get my e-mail?
M: No. I haven't been at work for a few days. Is he OK?
F: He sounded all right, but we didn't chat for long.

5 What is the date of the marathon?
M: ... and now a quick reminder about next month's marathon. The final date for runners to send in their application forms is the twentieth – sorry, but anyone applying after that date won't be considered. The big day is of course the twenty-eighth. Don't forget the minimum age is 18 and please enclose your fee with your application. All money goes to charity!

6 What's the weather going to be like tomorrow?
M: I don't think we should go to the beach tomorrow.
F: Why? It's not going to rain, is it? I thought they said it's going to be hotter than today!
M: That's right, and I don't want to burn.
F: But it's our last chance! There's going to be a storm at the weekend.

7 What are they going to eat tonight?
F: I'm really hungry! Shall we go out tonight?
M: I've already cooked the chicken!
F: But there's a new Italian restaurant just opened on the High Street! I've heard they do great pizza! We could have chicken salad tomorrow!
     All right. I'll put it in the fridge.

Tapescript

Questions 8–13
You will hear someone talking about summer activities. For each question, put a tick in the correct box.

M:
... and now let's look at some of the best things going on in our town in July. From the fifteenth to the eighteenth, the travelling Triple Theatre Company will be entertaining our children in the River Concert Hall. (8) Activities include storytelling, drama, and art. After last year's disappointing last-minute cancellation, I'm sure we're all really looking forward to what the company has to offer.
(9) Don't miss a great night out on Saturday 18th. The first of the Open Air Concerts in the Park starts off with music from the 80's. The fun starts at eight and goes on until midnight, when the show ends with a fantastic firework display. The concerts continue throughout the summer.
The second one in July is on 31st. There's more outdoor entertainment with Talk Theatre's performance of Shakespeare's *Twelfth Night* at the Abbey Ruins on Saturday 25th. Bring an umbrella because this performance takes place whatever the (10) weather, but please note there is no performance on Friday because the company has made a booking mistake. The performance will be in another town on that day! If you've bought a ticket for Friday, sorry, but you will be able to have a refund. There are several things happening along the river this (11) month, including a weekend water festival with a mystery band appearing on the evening of Friday 24th to start things off. They'll sail down the river at around 9 o'clock and will stay on board for their whole performance. All events take place around the river by Orkland Bridge and include boat trips, races, music and a children's entertainment tent. Don't miss the town's talent show on Sunday 19th July. There are prizes for winners in the following groups: children, teenagers aged 13–17 and adults aged 18 and over. Your act must last a minimum of (12) ten minutes and a maximum of 15. Please return your entry forms any time before Friday 17th July. Forms can be found at the Royal Theatre. If you like classic black and white films, you'll love the all-night drive-in free film festival that takes place every year in the park. This year it's on Friday 10th and as usual the night begins at nine in the evening and ends at six the (13) following morning. For a change, there will be refreshments including drinks and snacks available all night instead of until midnight. But be warned, as you know this is a free event and it's sometimes cancelled if there's rain about!

Part 3

14 entrance
15 Thursday
16 978 5423
17 computers
18 salads
19 bookshop

A   12 C   13 A

Tapescript

Questions 14–19
You will hear somebody welcoming a group of international students to a college. For each question, fill in the missing information in the numbered space.

F:
Welcome to Highdown College. Firstly I'd like to say something about living arrangements. Most of you already have a place in one of our college flats. If you have any problems, please contact the accommodation office. **(14)** You'll find the office at the entrance to the college and it's open from nine until four Monday to **(15)** Friday. During the holidays it's open, mornings only, on Monday **(16)** and Thursday. However, if you have an emergency, you can contact somebody on 978 5423. Moving on now ... the college has excellent facilities to help you with your studies, including the Learning Resource Centre that has more than 50,000 library **(17)** books. There are also 50 computers so you can use the internet. There are plenty of places to eat at the college, like the Hungry **(18)** Café on the first floor where you can have snacks including sandwiches and salads , or, if you prefer a hot meal at a very **(19)** reasonable price you can go to the Food Hall. You'll find it next to the bookshop, on the ground floor. Otherwise, you can have a pub lunch in the students' bar. There are also machines around the college, where you can buy crisps, chocolate and drinks. Right, if anybody has any questions about these matters, or anything else, please stay behind now. I hope all of you enjoy your time at our college.

Part 4

20 B   21 B   22 B   23 B   24 A   25 A

Tapescript

Questions 20–25
Look at the six sentences for this part. You will hear a conversation between a girl, Jodie, and a boy, Harry, about exams. Decide if each sentence is correct or incorrect.
If it is correct, put a tick in the box under A for YES. If it is not correct, put a tick in the box under B for NO.

F: Hello Harry. You look terrible!
M: I don't feel great.
F: Is there something wrong? Have you been to the doctor's?
M: No, I'm not ill. I'm just a bit tired. I'm probably not sleeping enough.
F: You shouldn't go out so late then.
(20) M: I'm not going out at all actually. I'm too busy studying.
F: Studying? But the exams aren't for another two months yet!
(21) M: I know, but I've got a lot to do. I didn't do much last term. I wish I'd been more like you!
F: Well, yeah, I went to every lecture and I took lots of notes, but
(22) that doesn't mean I'll get good grades. At least you don't get nervous in exams like I do.
M: Have you started revising yet?
(23) F: Not yet. I'll probably start next week, but I'm not going to stay up all night doing it! That never does any good. I might work

until midnight a couple of times, but that's all. If you don't sleep enough, you can't concentrate and you don't learn anything. Anyway you should have a weekend off.
M: I don't think so. I can't afford the time.
F: Of course you can! Why don't you come to the cinema with me, or, better still, the gym? Look at you! You used to be really fit! And now you're pale and unhealthy!
(24) M: I know, I do need more exercise.
F: Maria's having a party this Saturday, why don't you come?
M: I can't.
F: Of course you can. It's only one night.
M: Yeah but then I'll go to bed late and I won't work on Sunday.
F: Harry, you've still got two months! One weekend won't matter.
(25) M: OK. OK. I'll come.
F: Definitely?
M: Definitely.
F: Great. And what about the cinema tonight?
M: No. I'm definitely not going to the cinema.

Paper 3 Speaking

(Suggested language and structures that may be needed to do the tasks.)

Part 2

go (out) for a meal: quiet/be able to chat
go to a nightclub: have fun/too noisy/too many people
go to the cinema: see a film/not be able to talk
stay at home: have a chance to chat/have something to eat/relax
go to the park: quiet and relaxing/sit outside/in the sun/if the weather is good

... would/wouldn't be a good idea because ...
I think it would be good/best to ...

Part 3

Photo 1: winter/snow/ice/cold/freezing/looks beautiful/go walking/ice skating/do winter sports
Photo 2: summer/hot/sunny/relax/shade/dry/try to stay cool

Part 4

spring/summer/autumn/winter
The weather is cold/hot/mild.
It's sunny/freezing/rainy.
It often/sometimes/usually/nearly always rains/snows.
You can/(don't) have to wear ...
You can play/go to/enjoy ...
I prefer ... because
My favourite time of year is ...
I really don't like ...
I look forward to ...

Test 5

Paper 1 Reading and Writing

Reading

Part 1

1 B   2 C   3 B   4 A   5 B

Part 2

(The key words from each person are given opposite the key words from the answers.)

6 G

Pablo	Salsa for Beginners
keep him fit	dancing is great exercise
try … before making a final decision	our free Salsa for Beginners/ book onto one of our courses after that

7 B

Sally	Pen to Paper
works a lot of hours	home-study course
do something creative	make the most of your ability
in her own time	when and where you want

8 D

Maria	Lunchtime Fun
activity during the day	in your lunch hour
enjoys team games	basketball
keen to play regularly	every Tuesday and Thursday

9 H

Robert	On Stage
contact with other people	we have a lot of fun
enjoys performing	put on two shows a year

10 C

Helen	Mind and Body
a way of relaxing	help you deal with life's worries
can also do at home	something you can do anywhere
wants to look better and feel better	improve the way you look

Part 3

11 **B Incorrect.** It is not broken into several parts because it is *the largest remaining piece of unbroken rainforest* (l.2).

12 **A Correct.** They can only be found in the Great Bear Rainforest because *they don't exist anywhere else in the world* (l.7).

13 **A Correct.** You can have various kinds of holiday including *bear and whale watching … diving, snorkelling and fishing* (l.9).

14 **A Correct.** People who live in the area welcome tourists because *tourism is encouraged by local people* (l.11).

15 **B Incorrect.** The bears appear when the fish are returning *from the Pacific Ocean to the streams and rivers* (l.14).

16 **B Incorrect.** Knight Inlet is not in the middle of the rainforest because it is *on the southern edge of the Great Bear Rainforest* (l.17).

17 **B Incorrect.** Guests do not travel straight to the river by boat because they *board a small bus … to the river* (l.19).

18 **A Correct.** There is a choice of places to see the bears from because there are *five different viewing platforms, in three different areas* (l.20).

19 **B Incorrect.** Tourists cannot watch the bears all year round because they only wake up in April after *their winter sleep* (l.23).

20 **B Incorrect.** Tourists must sleep *one night in one of the two hotels there* (l.30) but not more than one night.

Part 4

(The first answer given is always the correct one.)

21 **C** The writer describes how her addiction grew.
A x She says that shopping was a problem for her and that she stopped going.
B x She says how much money she spent to show how addicted she was to shopping but it isn't the main aim.
D x She talks about buying clothes but not about fashion.

22 **C** She says *I carried on spending all my spare money on clothes – even after I had got married* (l.3).
A She says she didn't try to stop until her daughter asked why she had so many handbags (l.13).
B She used to spend all her spare wages on clothes and after she got married she carried on (l.3).
D She didn't realise she had a problem at first and when she did she couldn't believe it (l.14) but she doesn't say she got depressed.

23 **D** She says she *bought three pairs of boots, even though I already had another ten pairs at home* (l.9). She also had seventy-five handbags (l.13).
A x We don't know if the clothes were expensive, only that she bought a lot of them. She had a staff discount when she was a teenager (l.2).
B x She says sometimes, *she'd just buy the first thing I saw* (l.8).
C x She says she *used to go shopping every weekend* (l.5), not every day.

24 **A** She says she didn't realise she had a problem and *I couldn't believe what I'd done* (l.14).
B She doesn't say she was embarrassed.
C She doesn't say she was angry with herself.
D She doesn't say she was miserable.

25 **C** We know that she had a problem and she succeeded in fighting it by throwing away her credit card and not going shopping (l.16–18). She starts the text by saying *Shopping used to be my favourite activity* (l.1) so we know it isn't any more.
A We don't know what she looked like in the clothes she wore.
B She didn't fail, she succeeded in changing herself.
D She doesn't say that she had no money left, just that she spent a lot.

Part 5

26 C
This is a zero conditional so needs *if*. A, B and D have the wrong meaning.
27 C
A would mean *too* if it was *as well* but is in the wrong position. B is in the wrong position. D has the wrong meaning here.
28 A
B and D are followed by *into* to mean 'become'. C is not the right meaning.
29 B
A has the wrong meaning here. C and D are similar in meaning but not right here.
30 A
B, C and D are not followed by *to have*.
31 D
which is the correct pronoun in a non-defining relative clause referring to a place as subject.
32 C
already means 'by that time'. A and D are used in questions and negatives. B has the wrong meaning here.
33 A
put off means 'postpone'. B, C and D are all phrasal verbs but with the wrong meaning here.
34 B
at first means 'in the beginning'. A, C and D all make phrases with *at* but with the wrong meanings here.
35 D
A, B and C do not make phrases with *film*.

Writing

Part 1

1 That café has **the best** food in the area.
2 It isn't warm **enough** to go for a walk.
3 That cinema **has (got)** three screens.
4 You are not **allowed** to have your phones turned on during the performance.
5 You can only get a discount **if you are/you're** a student.

Part 2

Question 6: sample answer

Dear Jim,
how are you? I'm fine. I'm in Italy and I have visited the beautiful city of Nord Italy. Where are you now? Are you again in your country's home? I hope that you stay to fun with other friends and specially your girlfriend.
If you want, I wuold meet you to speak my adventures in Italy. Now I must go, because I must go to a pizzeria.
Bye Bye
Onofrio

COMMENTS
2 marks
One part to the question is not answered (he does not say what he is doing). Onofrio has apparently misunderstood the second part to the question and he asks his friend what <u>he</u> is doing rather than telling him about his own activities. The other parts to the question are dealt with less than adequately – Onofrio does not suggest that he is on holiday or mention his return.

Onofrio has written 70 words, which is well over the word limit, and has included three sentences which are irrelevant to the task.

Part 3

Question 7: sample answer

Late in the evening I heard a loud knock on the door. I was sleeping, but I woke up and when I went to open the door, I saw Laura, an old friend that I didn't see her since five years. Immediately I kissed her and I invited her to enter in my home. In the house there was a mess but I didn't think it, because I was seeing only Laura. She told me that she couldn't stay without me because she loves me. When I hear that, I kissed Laura but, after that, I woke up: it was only a dream!

COMMENTS
5 marks
This story is well-organised and shows confident use of language. There is good use of verb tenses and linking devices, e.g., *I was sleeping but I woke up ... and when ... I saw ...*, *She told me that she ...* , *but, after that, I woke up ...* . There is some good use of vocabulary, e.g. *kissed, mess, dream*. There are minor errors due to ambition, e.g.*didn't see her since five years, I didn't think it, stay without me* but the meaning is always clear.

Question 8: sample answer

Dear Mark,
Thanks for your letter and, like you asked to me, I'm going to tell you about my family. In the family we are 4: me, my sister of 17 years that is a student like me, my father Marco of 47 that is a manager and my mother Raffaella of 44 years that is an interviuwer. And there is also my little dog Withe of 5 years. Really we don't spend much time all togher but when we do it we enjoyed ourselves. I spend most of time with my sister, she's very funny, but less with my parents because they work a lot. Would you speak to me about your family too? I'm waiting for your answer!
Lot of affect
Caterina

COMMENTS
5 marks
This is a very good attempt which requires no effort by the reader. The letter is well organised and shows confident use of language. There is a wide range of structures and vocabulary, e.g. *There is also, We don't spend much time ... but when we do, I spend most of my time ...*, *less with my parents because ...*, *manager, interviewer*. Errors are mostly due to ambition and they do not cause problems for the reader, e.g. *of 17 years, my father that is*.

Paper 2 Listening

Part 1

1 C   2 B   3 C   4 A   5 A   6 B   7 C

Tapescript

Questions 1–7
There are seven questions in this part. For each question there are three pictures and a short recording. Choose the correct picture and put a tick in the box below it.

Example: How does the woman travel to work?
M: Did you buy that car you were interested in?
F: I decided I couldn't afford it and anyway there's nowhere to park near work. I'm going to carry on getting the bus and maybe buy a bike sometime.
M: That's a good idea. Cycling is a very healthy option!

1 What will the weather be like tomorrow?
F: ... after a rather dull and cloudy start to the day, we've seen a little sunshine this afternoon which we can expect to continue for most of tomorrow although by Friday it's bad news again as the rain clouds return just in time for the weekend.

2 How did Sarah get home last night?
M: I didn't see you leave the party last night Sarah. I thought you were getting the train with James at twelve?
F: I was so tired that I decided to get an earlier bus.
M: Did you have to wait long?
F: Well, in the end Pete drove past the bus stop and I got a lift with him.

3 What would the man like to do on his birthday?
F: How about going out for a meal on your birthday? We could go to that Chinese restaurant on Main Street.
M: Just you and me?
F: I thought we could ask some friends as well, unless you fancy staying in. I could cook for us all.
M: Don't worry, a meal out would be great. I'll ring Anna and Karl.

4 Which book did the woman buy?
M: Did you find that cookery book you wanted for your mum's birthday?
F: Yes, I did, but I found a much more interesting book on art history which I decided she'd prefer. It's all about French artists. She's been studying them at her art class recently. I'll get her the cookbook another time.

5 What time does the supermarket close today?
M: Good evening. It's now 6.45, so may I ask you to finish your shopping and start making your way to the checkouts, as there are only fifteen minutes left until the store closes at seven. May I remind you that next month the store will be closing every day at its new later time of eight o'clock. Our morning opening time of nine o'clock will remain the same. Thank you for shopping at Freeway.

6 Where is Mary?
M: Have you seen Mary? I thought I had a meeting with her today.
F: She's off to Italy for a one-day conference, isn't she?
M: That's next week.
F: Then she must be at the other office then. That's right, it's computer training.

7 Where are they going to meet?
M: Shall I pick you up from home tomorrow?

F: Well, I'm going to be at the library until eight so we could meet in town.
M: I can pick you up from the library, then you won't have to get a bus.
F: Thanks. That would be great.

Part 2

8 A   9 B   10 B   11 C   12 A   13 A

Tapescript

Questions 8–13
You will hear an interview with an organiser at a tennis club. For each question, put a tick in the correct box.

F: Today on *What's On Around Town*, I'm talking to Chris Jackson, one of the organisers at our local Eversham Tennis Club,
(8) who's here to try to convince you to become members. Chris, are you only interested in talented players or can anyone join?
M: Playing competitive tennis isn't all we do, although we have had some great successes and our level of teaching is very high. The club is also somewhere people can come to have fun. If you want to play for fun, it's best to come on a club night.
F: What are club nights?
M: Well, they're evenings for adult players that include playing tennis matches in a relaxed atmosphere rather than trying to improve skills. The club nights are held every Wednesday and Friday from 6 p.m. throughout the summer months.
(9) In the winter the courts are covered so that play can continue, but there's an extra fee to cover the cost of the extra lighting. It's not very much though. On Friday nights food and drinks are available at the end of play.
F: That's for adults, what about younger players?
(10) M: We have an excellent teaching programme run by Jack Stevens and his team that covers all ages and includes both individual and group sessions. The courses run for 10 weeks at a time and are open to members and non-members. Full payment in advance is preferred, although a weekly fee is possible.
Interviewer: Is there a club night for juniors?
(11) M: Oh yes. It's on Thursdays all year round. In fact, we're opening a small shop in the clubhouse selling snacks and cold drinks for this event, but that won't be until next spring. Any parents, by the way, who'd like to help out with that are very welcome.
(12) F: Are the people who run the club nights paid?
M: No. They are run by members and as you can imagine, there's a lot of work involved. There is an excellent teaching staff available and also one person in the office who comes in for a few hours a week to make sure everything runs smoothly.
F: And a final word on competitions. Do you encourage players to take part in wider competitions?
M: Definitely. We have a strong tradition of success in competitions in the area, and we prepare players for them through our own club competitions. The junior competition takes place in May.
F: How serious is that?
(13) M: It's a fun event but also a good opportunity for juniors of all levels to try out their tennis skills in a more competitive atmosphere. There's no fee for these club competitions, and winners are offered free extra lessons.

Part 3

14 50
15 afternoon
16 three/3-course meal
17 one/1 week
18 dance music
19 office

Tapescript

Questions 14–19
You will hear somebody talking about trips on the river.
For each question, fill in the missing information in the numbered space.

F:
Are you thinking of having a celebration but aren't sure what to do or where to go? River Cruises offer an original and popular place to celebrate any event, and it is perfect for office parties. We have boats available 12 months of the year to entertain (14) groups of between 10 and 50 people. . Trips are usually between (15) two and five hours, and can take place in the evening or (16) afternoon. We can supply a delicious buffet or alternatively our staff can formally serve you a three-course meal – all prepared on board of course by our top chefs. However, (17) we do ask you to order your meal at least one week before the event. Please feel free to talk to us in order to arrange the perfect atmosphere for your party. With fifteen years' experience, we are able to make suggestions to suit any mood or occasion. (18) The price of hiring the boat includes a disco or dance music. We can also supply live entertainment at an extra cost, which varies from jazz bands to a comedy show or magician. You can book through our website or by telephone. (19) Alternatively you can come to our office, which is situated in the Lochmead Leisure centre. Our office is at the back of the centre by the bar, and our staff will be very happy to discuss your arrangements.

Part 4

20 B   21 B   22 B   23 A   24 B   25 A

Tapescript

Questions 20–25
Look at the six sentences for this part. You will hear a conversation between a girl, Maria, and a boy, Dominic, about keeping fit. Decide if each sentence is correct or incorrect. If it is correct, put a tick in the box under A for YES. If it is not correct, put a tick in the box under B for NO.

F: I need some exercise. Any suggestions?
M: How about running?
F: Do you go running?
M: No, but I might start if I had someone to go with. I've always (20) liked the idea of doing a marathon. All that training must be fun.
F: Fun? Hard work more like. Anyway I don't want to get that fit, I just want to feel a bit healthier.
M: OK. We'll forget the marathon training then.
(21) F: Yeah, but running's a good idea actually. I've had enough of boring exercise classes.

M: I didn't know you did classes.
(22) F: I only went once or twice. I found it really embarrassing exercising in front of other people.
M: That's a shame. It takes a while before you get used to doing something like that and classes are a good place to meet people.
F: It just wasn't me.
(23) M: But you won't like running in the street if you don't like people watching you!
F: Well, if we went together I think I'd feel OK!
(24) M: Yeah and if we make an arrangement I'll have to turn up. I can imagine myself turning off the alarm clock and going back to sleep if I'm not meeting anybody.
F: So, we're going in the morning then?
M: Oh yeah. We won't want to go running after a hard day at college.
F: I suppose so. I'm not very good at getting up in the mornings though.
(25) M: Well, if you want to get healthy, you've got to work at it. You won't get anywhere if you stay in bed all day!
F: OK. OK.
M: Right. Let's start tomorrow. I'll see you at 6 o'clock at the park.
F: 6 o'clock in the morning?
M: Yes! In the morning!

Paper 3 Speaking

(Suggested language and structures that may be needed to do the tasks.)

Part 2

books: more/new books for the library/replace old ones
snack/drinks/sweet machine: useful/cheap/expensive/convenient
TV and video (player): interesting lessons/one for every classroom/modern equipment
tables/chairs: new ones/more comfortable/enough for everyone
computer and DVDs: use the internet/useful for studying

… would be a good/the best idea because …
We already have/there already is/are (enough) …
… would improve the school most.

Part 3

Photo 1: shopping centre/all kinds of shops/places to eat/crowded/on different floors/levels/more choice /cheaper
Photo 2: local shop/tables full of fruit and vegetables/a few customers/more expensive/less choice

Part 4

Shops: shopping centres/local shops/supermarkets/superstores/shoe shops/clothes shops/boutiques/music shops

I buy my … at …
I usually go shopping at the weekend/in the evenings.
I (don't really) like shopping for … because …
There is more/there isn't much choice at/in …
You can find whatever/everything you need …

General Mark Schemes for Writing

Part 2

Mark	Criteria
5	All content elements covered appropriately. Message clearly communicated to reader.
4	All content elements adequately dealt with. Message communicated successfully, on the whole.
3	All content elements attempted. Message requires some effort by the reader. **or** One content element omitted but others clearly communicated.
2	Two content elements omitted, or unsuccessfully dealt with. Message only partly communicated to reader. **or** Script may be slightly short (20 – 25 words).
1	Little relevant content and/or message requires excessive effort by the reader, or short (10 – 19 words).
0	Totally irrelevant or totally incomprehensible or too short (under 10 words).

Part 3

Band	Criteria
5	Very good attempt: • Confident and ambitious use of language. • Wide range of structures and vocabulary within the task set. • Well organised and coherent, through use of simple linking devices. • Errors are minor, due to ambition and non-impeding. Requires no effort by the reader.
4	Good attempt: • Fairly ambitious use of language. • More than adequate range of structures and vocabulary within the task set. • Evidence of organisation and some linking of sentences. • Some errors, generally non-impeding. Requires only a little effort by the reader.
3	Adequate attempt: • Language is unambitious, or if ambitious flawed. • Adequate range of structures and vocabulary. • Some attempt at organisation; linking of sentence not always maintained. • A number of errors may be present, but are mostly non-impeding. Requires some effort by the reader.
2	Inadequate attempt: • Language is simplistic/limited/repetitive. • Inadequate range of structures and vocabulary. • Some incoherence; erratic punctuation. • Numerous errors, which sometimes impede communication. Requires considerable effort by the reader.
1	Poor attempt: • Severely restricted command of language. • No evidence of range of structures and vocabulary. • Seriously incoherent; absence of punctuation. • Very poor control; difficult to understand. Requires excessive effort by the reader.
0	Achieves nothing: language impossible to understand, or totally irrelevant to task.

(The band score for Part 3 is translated to a mark out of 15.)

Band	Criteria
5	**Very good attempt:** • Confident and ambitious use of language. • Wide range of structures and vocabulary within the task set. • Well organised and coherent, through use of simple linking devices. • Errors are minor, due to ambition and non-impeding. Requires no effort by the reader.
4	**Good attempt:** • Fairly ambitious use of language. • More than adequate range of structures and vocabulary within the task set. • Evidence of organisation and some linking of sentences. • Some errors, generally non-impeding. Requires only a little effort by the reader.
3	**Adequate attempt:** • Language is unambitious, or if ambitious flawed. • Adequate range of structures and vocabulary. Some attempt at organisation; linking of sentence not always maintained. • A number of errors may be present, but are mostly non-impeding. Requires some effort by the reader.
2	**Inadequate attempt:** • Language is simplistic/limited/repetitive. • Inadequate range of structures and vocabulary. • Some incoherence; erratic punctuation. • Numerous errors, which sometimes impede communication. Requires considerable effort by the reader.
1	**Poor attempt:** • Severely restricted command of language. • No evidence of range of structures and vocabulary. • Seriously incoherent; absence of punctuation. • Very poor control; difficult to understand. Requires excessive effort by the reader.
0	Achieves nothing: language impossible to understand, or totally irrelevant to task.

Assessment

Throughout the test, candidates are assessed on their language skills, not their personality, intelligence or knowledge of the world. They must, however, be prepared to develop the conversation, where appropriate, and respond to the tasks set. Prepared speeches are not acceptable. Candidates are assessed on their own individual performance and not in relation to each other. Both examiners assess the candidates according to criteria which are interpreted at PET level. The interlocutor awards a mark for Global Achievement, whilst the assessor awards marks according to four analytical criteria: Grammar and Vocabulary, Discourse Management, Pronunciation and Interactive Communication.

Grammar and Vocabulary

This scale refers to the accurate and appropriate use of grammatical forms and vocabulary. It also includes the range of both grammatical forms and vocabulary. Performance is viewed in terms of the overall effectiveness of the language used in dealing with the tasks.

Discourse Management

This scale refers to the coherence, extent and relevance of each candidate's individual contribution. On this scale the candidate's ability to maintain a coherent flow of language is assessed, either within a single utterance or over a string of utterances. Also assessed here is how relevant the contributions are to what has gone before.

Pronunciation

This scale refers to the candidate's ability to produce comprehensible utterances to fulfil the task requirements. This includes stress, rhythm and intonation, as well as individual sounds. Examiners put themselves in the position of the non-language specialist and assess the overall impact of the pronunciation and the degree of effort required to understand the candidate. Different varieties of English, e.g. British, North American, Australian etc., are acceptable, provided they are used consistently throughout the test.

Interactive Communication

This scale refers to the candidate's ability to use language to achieve meaningful communication. This includes initiating and responding without undue hesitation, the ability to use interactive strategies to maintain or repair communication, and sensitivity to the norms of turn-taking.

Global Achievement

This scale refers to the candidate's overall effectiveness in dealing with the tasks in the four separate parts of the PET Speaking Test. The global mark is an independent, impression mark which reflects the assessment of the candidate's performance from the interlocutor's perspective. The interlocutor gives one global mark for each candidate's performance across all parts of the test.

Speaking Test Outline

Part 1 (2–3 minutes)

Phase 1

Interlocutor

A/B   Good morning/afternoon/evening. Can I have your mark sheets, please?
I'm …. and this is ….. He/She is just going to listen to us.

A   Now, what's your name? Thank you.

B   And what's your name? Thank you.

B   What's your surname? How do you spell it? Thank you.

A   And, what's your surname? How do you spell it? Thank you.

> (Back-up prompts)
> How do you write your family/second name?
> Have you got a job?
> What job do you do?
> What subject(s) do you study?

A   Where do you live/come from? Do you work or are you a student in …? What do you study?

B   *(Repeat as for A)*

Phase 2

Interlocutor
(One or more questions for each candidate)

Do you enjoy studying English? Why (not?)
Do you think that English will be useful for you in the future?
What did you do yesterday evening/last weekend?
What do you enjoy doing in your free time?
Thank you.

In the next part you are going to talk to each other.

Part 2 (2–3 minutes)

Interlocutor

A/B   I'm going to describe a situation to you. *(Task-specific rubric)* Here is a picture with some ideas to help you. *(Picture sheet 3 handed to candidates)*
I'll say that again. *(Repeat task-specific rubric)* All right? Talk together.

Thank you.

Part 3 (3 minutes)

Interlocutor

A/B   Now, I'd like each of you to talk on your own about something. I'm going to give each of you a photograph of *(task-specific rubric)*.
Candidate A, here is your photograph. *(Photo given to candidate A)*. Please show it to Candidate B, but I'd like you to talk about it. Candidate B, you just listen, I'll give you your photograph in a moment.
Candidate A, please tell us what you can see in your photograph.
Thank you. *(Retrieve photograph from Candidate A)*

Now, Candidate B, here is your photograph. It also shows *(task-specific rubric)*. *(Photo given to Candidate B)*. Please show it to Candidate A and tell us what you can see in the photograph.
Thank you. *(Retrieve photograph from Candidate B)*

Part 4 (3 minutes)

Interlocutor

A/B   Your photographs showed *(task-specific rubric)*.
Thank you. That's the end of the test.

OXFORD
UNIVERSITY PRESS

Great Clarendon Street, Oxford OX2 6DP

Oxford University Press is a department of the University of Oxford.
It furthers the University's objective of excellence in research,
scholarship, and education by publishing worldwide in

Oxford New York

Auckland Bangkok Buenos Aires Cape Town Chennai
Dar es Salaam Delhi Hong Kong Istanbul Karachi Kolkata
Kuala Lumpur Madrid Melbourne Mexico City Mumbai Nairobi
São Paulo Shanghai Taipei Tokyo Toronto

Oxford and Oxford English are registered trade marks of
Oxford University Press in the UK and in certain other countries

ISBN 0 19 453471 5

Printed in Spain by Unigraf S.L.

Acknowledgments

The publisher is grateful to the University of Cambridge Local
Examinations Syndicate for permission to reproduce material from the
PET handbook for the updated examination.

Illustrations by David Eaton.

Assessment of sample answers for Writing by Lucrecia Luque-Mortimer.

The author and publisher would like to thank Richard Udall and the
students at the British School in Bari, Italy for their help with the sample
answers.